PRAISE FC
AND *NONE... ... GAME PLAN*

"Matt may not have served in combat fighting overseas as a Navy SEAL, but what I can tell you is he applies the same level of drive, determination and steadfast commitment to his task at hand. His passion for helping others is contagious!" – Mark Owen, *New York Times* bestselling author of *No Easy Day* and *No Hero*

"Matt George has led a life of community leadership taking care of some of the most vulnerable people in our community. His caring and concern to improve the lives of our fellow citizens is exemplary and an example for all." – Ray LaHood, US Congressman for Illinois (1995-2008) and US Secretary of Transportation (2009-2013)

"Every community needs a Matt George fighting for them. His compassion for the kids and families is next to none. He's a true leader. I want him on my team." – Jim McMahon, NFL Quarterback and two-time Superbowl Champion

"Every day, I hear about all these people that say, 'I want to do something to help my community.' Matt George doesn't say that—he gets up and does it *every day*. There's a big difference between the two, and if you have any questions, watch Matt George. He does it." – Dan Hampton, NFL Hall of Famer and Superbowl Champion

"Matt has displayed exceptional passion embracing his craft of being a leader and building community bridges." – Andre Dawson, eight-time National League All-Star and National Baseball Hall of Famer

"Matt George is a master in the NGO world by leading in a very business oriented and collaborative way. He maximizes social impact in the community. Successful communities are the result of the best ROI in all sectors. Matt's leadership and lessons have greatly impacted the most underserved." – Michele Sullivan, former President of the Caterpillar Foundation and author of *Looking Up*

"Matt exemplifies leadership in his community and making it a much better place. He's involved, committed and is recognized for his many contributions. His ability to lead a large, complex organization is well documented and many look up to him as a result." – Douglas R. Oberhelman, former CEO and Executive Chairman of Caterpillar Inc.

To all the social service team members all over the world, who are heroes to so many—the impact on our children, families and communities is immeasurable

Foreword

I've only known Matt George for less than a year, but he's made an impression on me.

We met when I was a keynote speaker at a "Winning is Everything" conference in Las Vegas. The conference was focused on giving business and leadership advice to financial and accounting leaders. When it was over, I got off the stage, took a few pictures and headed off through a side door, ending up down by the escalators.

Right when I got there, there was Matt. He'd come to the conference with his father and planned his route carefully to catch me on my way out of the building. Because there are always a lot of people who want to talk after the conferences, I usually try to lose people before they follow me all the way back to my hotel room. But there was something about Matt, so I said I could give him two minutes.

"Kevin," he said to me, "I'm not even here for the event. I'm here because I knew I wanted to listen to you." When I speak at events, I'm typically getting approached by people who say, "Hey, thanks for speaking

—I have a product I want to sell," or "I have an idea I need funding for." But when Matt came up to me, he said he had something different than I was used to. "I don't have a product to pitch you," he said, "but I'm running a children's home and my kids need help."

I was in a rush, but Matt's persistence had caught my attention. "Listen," I told him. "I'm interested in speaking to you, but I need to get on a plane." I live in Florida and Matt lives in Illinois, but Matt said he'd be down in Sarasota soon. To make a long story short, he suggested we have lunch, and I said that would be fine. We exchanged phone numbers, and I went on my way.

When we met for a second time face-to-face soon after, I took an instant liking to him. Matt was clearly so focused on helping kids. It was a sincere passion for him. He told me about the hard things he was dealing with on a day to day basis, terrible things like violence, shootings, poverty, kids who didn't have parents or a place to sleep and so on. But what also struck me right away was his business mind.

Matt runs his nonprofit organization like a business, and it is very successful. I deal with a lot of nonprofits, and I'm on the board of one currently. Unfortunately, what I often see is a mentality that isn't focused on running them like businesses. Instead, it's more of a focus on trying to get handouts to keep the organizations going.

When I look at my own business deals, if I'm going to sell something or have someone write me a check, I need to know that there's something in it for them. What problem can I solve and how can I create that solution? In a lot of nonprofits, they lean too much on the sympathy card and think of themselves as "less than" or in need.

When it comes to Matt's organization, The Children's Home Association of Illinois, they operate within their means and retain enough funds to be able to overcome any funding gaps along the way, thereby having the ability to meet payroll and operational expenses. In the nonprofit world, that's pretty unheard of—so many of those organizations are running week-to-week or month-to-month. In his case, Matt is running his organization in a healthy way that retains enough capital and builds momentum, all of it targeted for that inevitable "rainy day," so to speak.

As a businessman myself, there are several things I do to give back to society. I started a nonprofit called EO, the Entrepreneurs Organization. We're in 150 cities and 55 countries, with 10,000 members paying $5,000 a year to be a part of it—and I don't see a dime of that. That's part of my giveback.

When Matt approached me, I knew he was a winning ticket. I have a certain budget in my life for helping people, and I knew that helping Matt would mean helping a lot of kids as well. Out of our meetings and many phone calls, I decided to offer him my mentorship.

I remember one of the first things I told him. "Listen, "I said, "you've created a bit of a profile for yourself in your community, but it's too small of a profile."

From my perspective, what Matt has done at Children's Home is so powerful that it needs to be shared. He needs to share it with other people so they can do the same thing in their organizations. He needs to use his accomplishments and his profile to "build the brand" of nonprofits in general, so to speak.

Although Matt is helping tons of people in his hometown, by becoming a speaker or a voice in the nonprofit world, he could end up helping 10 to 100 times that many. The work he's doing in Illinois is important and he ought to keep doing it—but I truly feel Matt George has a voice that can offer a ton of value to the whole world.

To realize that value, I told him he needed to build his own brand and find a way to control his own destiny. He needed to write a book. After a lot of effort and soul-searching, the book you're about to read is the result of conversations Matt and I had—and of a lot of work Matt put into it on his own.

I'm a busy man, and though I love to give back, I'm selective about the people I choose to support. With Matt George, it's a no-brainer. The nonprofit industry needs a stronger brand, but it also needs a stronger attitude. After seeing what Matt has accomplished and what an outstanding guy he is, I know he's the right man for that mission. In my opinion, it may become the defining mission of his life.

But if anybody is going to change and save a lot of lives, it's going to be Matt George.

Kevin Harrington
Inventor of the infomercial, original Shark on *Shark Tank*, "As Seen on TV" pioneer

Table of Contents

Chapter 1:
How It All Started

Around hour 56, I started to hallucinate. I'd been playing doubles tennis for almost two-and-a-half days straight without sleeping. The psychologist I'd talked to before I started told me this would happen. I knew I had to stay focused just on what was right in front of me, not even on returning all the balls or winning every match. Just on making it all the way through to the end.

In the middle of it, I didn't know I was on a tennis court anymore. I thought I was shopping in a grocery store. Then I thought I was sitting in class at the University of Illinois. A minute later, I could've sworn I was sitting at my grandma's house on the couch. All these thoughts were swirling through my brain.

But a second later, my mind would be sharp again. *You're Matt George*, I said to myself, *and you're setting a world record for playing non-stop doubles tennis*. I wasn't even halfway to the standing world record yet, but I knew I had to keep going. Even if my vision was getting blurry and the blisters in my palms were raw and bursting around the racket handle.

I had to finish. Not for the glory or to say I did it, but because doing it would get a lot of attention, and the attention would bring a lot of dollars, and the dollars would help out one little girl who needed help. A little girl named Stephanie was the real reason for all of it. Even aside from the money, having Stephanie see all these people gathered to support her would boost her spirits—and those of her family and even the community. With all that positivity and support, how could she not fight through and keep going?

But I'm getting ahead of myself.

For the first 18 years of my life, I grew up in Danville, Illinois, a little town near the Indiana border on the east side of the state. It was a manufacturing town with a lot of factories that ended up gradually leaving over the years. Even though the town dwindled over time, I was always proud to be from Danville. It was one of those towns that everybody would rip on with the usual smart-aleck comments. *Why would you want to live there?* To tell the truth, that small town instilled a lot of the beliefs I still have today, namely that you should do right by other people and that the members of a small community ought to do their best to take care of one another.

I had a basically normal midwestern upbringing with good parents who always stressed the importance of taking care of others. It didn't matter what it was—

sometimes it was holding the door for other people and other times it was just tucking in your shirt.

Above all, it was about doing the right thing.

Maybe as a result of that, I knew very early on that I wanted to help people. I hated seeing people being bullied or made fun of, and I was the first to stick up for anybody who was in trouble. It always bothered me when people who didn't have the loudest voices got silenced by other people who did. I thought that I was supposed to protect those people.

Even though I would speak up for people and feel guilty about things that were happening around me, I didn't realize how big of an impact I could make when I was just a kid. As I got a little older, I started seeing what real life was about. I began seeing crises in my town and people in need, and I always wanted to do more.

I just didn't know how to go about doing it. That was the first turning point for me—for my job, for my career and for what I now consider my calling.

From Tennis to Saving Lives

Life in Danville was fine and comfortable, but it was pretty unexciting. I mostly did what my parents told me, hung out with my friends and bonded with my dad over baseball. Like any little boy, my dad was my mentor and idol. But he was also my baseball coach. From the very beginning, I was obsessed with baseball and we would always play together. It was the all-American small-town life.

But that all changed when I was 11.

My parents weren't getting along anymore and after trying to work it out for a while, they decided to get a divorce. Though my dad was still going to be a force and a presence in our lives, he left the house. My siblings and I couldn't grasp what had happened and we didn't understand what had gone on between my parents. It was a strange time in our home and everybody was confused. But after a while, I was just angry.

That anger turned pretty quickly into me not liking a lot of things and people.

I started getting rude with people and having an attitude. Maybe most of all, I started doing a lot worse in school than I had before. Up until that point, I'd been a straight-A student. With everything that was going on, my grades started dropping to Bs, Cs and even Ds. One day in fifth grade, I was getting lippy with one of my teachers and he threatened to call my dad. Without missing a beat, I rattled off the phone number to call. After that, I was sent to the principal's office to have a chat with him about my attitude.

Though I never really failed any of my classes, it was clear I just didn't care about them. And that attitude was starting to extend into other areas of my life as well. About a year after that, my mom got remarried and my stepdad came into the picture. My dad was my hero—and he still is today. Nowadays, he remains my mentor and a great friend. But back then, I was upset with him.

My stepdad came along at the perfect time, and one of the first things he did was introduce me to tennis. I was an athletic kid and immediately locked into the sport. My stepdad and I spent time running drills together, hitting the ball back and forth and generally getting to know one another. All the time I spent with my stepdad meant that he was becoming a big part of my life and a big part of my family.

Because I was still angry and mourning, I decided to turn my back on my old interests. I quit baseball. From then on, I was going to be all about tennis.

Tennis became my outlet. I joined a local tennis club and practiced at 6 am every Tuesday, Thursday and Saturday along with a group of other kids my age. Every day, my routine was the same: get through school, then go play tennis. When the weekend rolled around, I would go play tennis. Anytime I had nothing to do, I played tennis.

There was a tennis pro that worked at our tennis club who was a great player and coach. One day, he and his brother set out to break the Guinness World Record for continuous doubles play. To break the record, you and a partner would have to play doubles tennis for 122 hours. You could accumulate five minutes of rest time after every hour you played. You were also allowed to bank those five-minute increments if you chose. And that's what they did.

They followed through on their strategy and succeeded in breaking the world record, setting a new one at 125 hours straight. I could not have been more impressed. I was in complete awe at how their bodies could handle five straight days of playing a sport with such limited down time.

What would drive somebody to accomplish something like that? I wondered.

The big turning point for me came when I was 16. I was relatively close with a friend who was in a handful of my high school classes. We were in an outdoor-oriented youth program together called Indian Guides, which was run through the YMCA. It was basically a Boy Scouts-esque program where the fathers were involved. Though not every meeting was the same, the basic gist was that everyone got together to do nature activities. I knew my friend's dad was a police officer, and I also knew how kind his mom and younger brother were.

One day, my friend just didn't show up for class. I'd heard around school that he wasn't doing well, that he was going through some personal health issues. I figured he was just under the weather and that he'd be back in no time. The next day, his seat was empty again. I found out later that day he died.

He'd been a straight-A student who sat in the front row, right next to me. I'd been put in the front row of the class for a different reason. The teachers thought they could keep a better eye on me that way. After he was gone, I kept looking over to my right and seeing his chair empty, never to be filled again.

At that point in life, my parents had split, I was struggling in school and I was mourning it all. But this put my problems in perspective.

I remember when I was nine years old, my grandpa passed away. He'd been 70 years old when he died, and everybody around me had kept saying how young *he* was. Seven years later, my friend died at the age of 16. I didn't think something like that could happen. It taught me that death was a real thing and it was indiscriminate. It was a kick in the gut to try to comprehend that.

I remember lying in bed at night, trying to figure out what I could do for my friend's family. I knew I needed to help, but I couldn't figure out how. I thought about my life, my days at the tennis club and my coaches, and then it hit me.

My coaches had broken the world record for playing tennis doubles, I reasoned. *Why couldn't I do the same?* Just like the coaches had done, I would play doubles tennis for as long as I could.

And I would turn it into a fundraiser for my friend's family.

To be clear, I had no idea whether they actually needed the money or not. Either way, I felt like they could probably do something with it. My thinking went like this: *I know it's going to cost a lot of money for a funeral. I don't know how any of that works, but if I can raise just a little money for the family, it would be a nice thing to do. It would mean a lot to them.*

I went around town and explained to everybody what my mission was and how I would play as much tennis as I could for as long as I could against whoever wanted to play me. All I asked was that each person make a small donation or sponsor me for every hour I played.

Sure enough, the big day came. And I was determined to play my heart out.

With different partners coming in and out by my side, I played tennis for hours and hours, to the point of becoming delirious. I fought as hard as I could, but by hour 62, my mind was playing mental tricks because of the sleep deprivation. I was frustrated that I'd failed to hit the high goal I'd set for myself but it wasn't a complete loss. When all was said and done, I'd helped raise more than $3,000 for my friend's family.

I remember surprising them by going over to their house and presenting them the check, along with the tennis racket I used. The moment was so emotional for the family, but it ended up hitting me just as hard. It meant so much more to me than just the effort I'd put in. It made me think of other things, other ways I could make an impact.

I knew that I truly had the power to help other people—and tennis was how I could do it.

In 1988, I realized my dream of becoming a tennis pro probably wasn't going to happen—but it still helped me go to Parkland Junior College in Champaign, Illinois on a tennis scholarship. Though I was proud of myself, I knew I needed to start thinking of a different career path. My whole family was pretty athletic, but my first cousin Jeff George was preternaturally gifted.

Jeff had been oddly famous since he was in about eighth grade. When he was a freshman, he was the '86 USA Today and Gatorade High School Football Player of the Year. As a senior in high school, he was already signing autographs. He was the only number-one draft pick from the University of Illinois *ever* — and that includes some pretty big names.

That trend continued as he got older. Jeff was a gun-slinging quarterback, a top baseball and basketball player and a very popular figure at the University of Illinois. He also became my college roommate. As I quickly learned from rooming with Jeff, there were certain opportunities and advantages that came from being (or being around) a popular athlete.

For whatever reason, people are drawn to the aura of sports stars. Maybe it's their positive attitude or level of achievement — who knows. All I knew was that I could surf on the wave that was swelling around Jeff. I took advantage of it to shake hands and meet people. I considered how my sports career had already led to some significant fundraising.

Someday, I figured, this may turn into a job.

Sometime later, I was driving in Champaign-Urbana when I heard a local radio spot. The story was about a seven-year-old girl named Stephanie who had leukemia. The radio show was about 30 minutes long and I drove around aimlessly, listening to the entire thing. The program was explaining all the hard times she and her family were going through. It was highlighting just how tough it was to fight that disease.

For whatever reason, hearing that story that day completely broke my heart. I pulled over to the side of the road and let the sadness wash over me, feeling the pain of Stephanie's story deep in my bones.

It stuck with me the next day and the day after that. The memory of it just wouldn't go away. Somewhere nearby, there was a little girl named Stephanie who was suffering. And here I was, an able-bodied young college student. Everything in the world was ahead of me, while everything for her was in danger of being taken away. Having come across her story, how could I not do something to help? Before the radio show was over, I had scrawled her name down on a piece of paper.

I vividly remember comparing that scrap of paper to the phone book, scanning for Stephanie's name, phone number and address. After writing a few potential entries down, I called them one by one, gradually eliminating them from my list. Everybody I talked to that day must've thought I was crazy—but I was just determined.

I eventually got in touch with Stephanie's mom and told her I had an idea of how to help. It was a decision that changed the course of my life forever.

On September 23rd, 1991, I organized a local press conference to make an important announcement. I was partnering with The Leukemia Society and I was going to make another attempt at what I couldn't do when I was 16. I was going to break the world record for non-stop doubles tennis. Once again, it would be a huge fundraiser and all the money raised would go to defeating leukemia and honoring this little girl.

Beating the record would require me to play tennis for 125 hours straight.

Since the first time I'd attempted the record, I had grown so much. I'd gone for 62 hours the first time and now I knew the challenges that awaited me. *This time*, I told myself, *I'll make all the necessary preparations*. I'd be ready for the hallucinations, the pains, the fatigue and the blisters. I would talk to coaches and professionals, I would talk to sports psychologists, I would talk to anybody who would help me achieve my goal.

My entire motivation was to help Stephanie as much as I could.

Similar to the fundraiser I'd organized before, each doubles player who wanted to play against or with me would pay a certain fee. With fees and sponsorships, I figured I could raise a good chunk of change.

When the day finally came, it was just as hard as I thought it would be.

The first 12 hours blew by, even up to the first 24. I kept playing and playing, banking my five-minute breaks, resting for a little bit and getting back up again. Though my doubles partners kept switching out, I was the one constant while time passed around me indefinitely. At 56 hours, I was hallucinating—still, I pushed on. I cleared my previous plateau of 62 hours.

There was no going back now.

Time began to lose meaning. All that was left was pain, extreme mental and physical pain—the hardest I've ever had to endure. Towards the end, things started going seriously wrong. I got physically ill. My shoulders started seizing up and crunching around in their joints. My hip popped out of place. At a certain point, the pain of the blisters on my hand became indescribable.

After some amount of time, I nearly collapsed. I decided to take a five.

Right away, my brother ran up to me and asked if I was okay. I told him how nauseous I felt, that I really was starting to think about quitting. I was disoriented and didn't know how close I was to the end—I just knew it was a lot closer than I'd made it last time.

"You can't quit," my brother said sternly. With that, he disappeared for a moment. Just a second later, he reappeared on the sidelines. As I looked up to meet his eyes, there was Stephanie standing beside him, staring right into my eyes and smiling.

That immediately brought me out of my funk.

I got back on my feet and back in the game. By the end, I'd played tennis for five grueling days and a total of 1,845 matches.

In all, I'd played 126 hours straight of doubles tennis—and I'd raised more than $30,000.

The feeling in the crowd was ecstatic, and to pull something this big off felt otherworldly. *This is definitely going to put a smile on the faces of all the kids out there battling cancer*, I thought. I'd finally accomplished something that I thought was nearly impossible. Well, I almost did.

As it turned out, my goal of making it into the *Guinness Book of World Records* never materialized.

The Leukemia Society hadn't really done their homework and research behind the entire event. A true doubles team—a team with the same two players the whole time—set the record I'd been trying to break. Though I'd played the entire time, my partners had been switching in and out around me. As a result, I wasn't eligible to be a world record holder.

Regardless, I knew only a few people in the world could've accomplished what I did—and the team and I had achieved the end result we wanted. That event got *national* attention, and that had always been the most important part of it.

Looking back, I realize all the stuff about the glory and the credit for the record was just immature thinking. In reality, that realization was the start of my life.

It was never about me after all. When I broke the record (on paper, anyway), I thought that was a milestone that would catapult me into playing tennis my entire life. Three years later, I not only gave up on the dream—I gave up on tennis rackets *completely*. Since the age of 25, I've probably only played tennis 10 times.

Here's the thing: at a certain point, I recognized I really wasn't as good as I thought.

I figured I could do more from appearances and from generating publicity. I was trying to be an influencer for good causes before that was even a real term. After all, there were probably about 50 news articles about me that rolled out after that fundraiser happened (even if you're not going to see many of them in a Google search today).

If I could keep doing these kinds of events and generating this kind of enthusiasm, I figured, I could really make a difference. I could take care of people, and I could change people's lives.

The Compassionate CEO

Now, I know what you're thinking. This book is called *Nonprofit Game Plan*, not *Matt George's Life Story*. Still, it's important for people to know where I'm coming from and what motivated me to do what I do.

It happened in a few distinct phases. On the one hand, I was growing up comfortably in Danville until my parents split and my world got shaken up. I had my moment of doubt and apathy—but hey, I was young. Right on the tail of that doubt were a couple of experiences that opened up my heart again. Those experiences are the bedrock of my entire life and business philosophy today.

I always say that my mission is changing and saving lives, and the seeds of that mission were already planted by my 16-year-old friend and with Stephanie. But Stephanie was particularly pivotal. What if I'd never heard her story on the radio that day? Who knows where I would've ended up? Fortunately, the end of that story is Stephanie beat her disease and I've always felt like I played a role in her recovery.

After Stephanie, my mission started taking shape. The story had been written up everywhere, so I was starting to become a recognizable name. People were calling in to ask if I could do such-and-such to raise money for their charity, or this-and-that to raise money for some other well-intended cause. I couldn't do everything, but I was honored. And I knew I had to capitalize on the momentum.

In 1990, my cousin Jeff was the number one overall draft pick in the NFL. He'd gone pro with the Indianapolis Colts, but I still had two more years before I was going to graduate. He came back in 1991, after a year in the pros, and moved back in with me for a summer to finish his degree. Because of Jeff's new "in" at the NFL, I figured there might be an angle to get access to some professional athletes.

As a kid and even up until I graduated, Walter Payton was one of my heroes.

He'd been a running back for the Chicago Bears and Mike Ditka called him the greatest football player he'd ever seen. Payton also had the Walter and Connie Payton Foundation on Golf Road in Schaumburg, Illinois, outside of Chicago and just a few hours away from Champaign. I knew I was going to keep doing tennis fundraisers all year, but I figured I could use some more star power to keep the eyeballs on us and the donations flowing in.

So one day, I said to myself, "I'm going to do an event with Walter Payton." Even though Jeff was in the NFL, it's not like he and Payton were best buds. Still, what little connection they had encouraged me to try.

I did everything I could to get in touch with him. I called him over and over again, I left messages and I harangued his office assistant. I told everybody that I was planning an event called Ace Leukemia. It was a tennis fundraiser and I wanted Walter Payton to be involved (even though he was a football star).

To make a long story short, I finally got through, and he called me at home one day.

"Hey Matt," Walter Payton said in his reedy voice, "do you think you could come down to my office and meet me?"

I couldn't believe that I'd actually gotten Walter Payton on the phone. Before long, I made the three-hour drive down to the foundation and stood face-to-face with my childhood hero.

"You're a persistent son of a gun," he said to me when I got there. "What do you want me for?"

So many thoughts were running through my head, but my ask was coming from a simple and direct place.

"Number one," I said, "I had all your posters in my room growing up because I loved the Chicago Bears. Number two, everybody where I'm from loves you — why wouldn't you want to come?"

Although he liked my energy and said he could make himself available, the fact of the matter was that Walter Payton still had a speaking and appearance fee.

But I had an idea for that.

One of my grandmas had given me $5,000 to use for books at school, which was a considerable sum of money. But I never bought a book that year. Instead of buying books for my classes, I used all of my book money to get Walter his down payment to come to Champaign for my fundraiser.

And just like that, I had organized Ace Leukemia with Walter Payton.

But the momentum didn't stop there.

After Jeff graduated and went back to the NFL, he started his own charitable foundation called the Jeff George Foundation and he put me in charge. By 1992, I had full access to Jeff and a bunch of other pro athletes and celebrities he knew. They would donate their time, gear, shoes and jerseys to us for fundraising events—along with money. Jeff played for the Indianapolis Colts from 1990 to 1993. After that, he got traded to the Atlanta Falcons.

As he moved around the country, so did I.

After moving to Atlanta in 1994, I started organizing more events for kids and adults dealing with various issues. It was everything from fundraising for cancer research to helping kids dealing with child abuse. For the most part, our events came out of seeing a terrible story on the news and saying: *I think we can help*. But the biggest thing we had going was the power and cachet of an NFL quarterback in our corner.

Around that same time, my cousin Jeff and I were starting to become pretty good friends with comedian Jeff Foxworthy. It was during the prime era of his "you might be a redneck" routine, and his star was definitely rising. We crossed paths at social events, and I mentioned to him that I was doing a little event back in Champaign again, one I'd done before to raise money for cancer research.

I followed the same persistent path I had with Walter Payton, and just a little while later, there I was at Ace Leukemia with Jeff Foxworthy. That was all before I was 24 years old.

I could go on and on.

In the 10 years from 1992 to 2002, I raised money in Atlanta, Indianapolis, Champaign and Danville. I started getting very good at putting on events and connecting the right people. I left Atlanta in 1997 to go back to Illinois, when Jeff got traded to the Raiders. Basically, I decided that I didn't want to move to Oakland, California.

It was around that time that I started reflecting a bit. I was almost 30, and I realized I didn't have a solid plan for the future. In the midst of all the star-studded events, I started to think I was straying from my mission just a little bit.

I really need to focus on getting back to the core of giving, I thought. After a little while, the time seemed right to break out to do some nonprofit work on my own as a free agent.

In 2004, I became the President and CEO of Youth Farm in Peoria, Illinois, an organization that offered residential services for homeless and at-risk kids. I worked there until 2008 when I transitioned over to the Cancer Center for Healthy Living, another nonprofit in Peoria that provided cancer services to those fighting the disease.

After six years working there, it was time for another change. In the time I'd been at the Cancer Center for Healthy Living, Youth Farm incorporated into a much bigger nonprofit called the Children's Home Association of Illinois (which is a story I'll save for a little later). Children's Home is one of the largest nonprofits in downstate Illinois.

In October 2014, I became CEO of Children's Home—and I'm still there.

Though I could go through my life and work experience in more detail, the point is that I was lucky to have the experiences I had in the order I did. Going from high school to college, my purpose was clear to me: I could combine my sports and social skills with that heart-level drive to help people.

And if I did it correctly, I could make real changes in people's lives.

While it's important in life to be selfless and giving, I've learned over the years that being truly selfless can still be very selfish—and that's not necessarily a bad thing. When I was young, I wanted to stand out. I wanted to prove myself and to be a leader in my community while I was helping people. As it turned out, that quality ended up working in my favor.

My mission was always to help people and save lives, but my character and connections attracted other people to my mission as well. Using what made me and the people around me unique, we built something much larger than the sum of the parts. Today, I'm fortunately a little bit less about me, and I'm more of a team player than I was when I was a young adult. But the principle remains the same.

People have certain ideas about what it means to be a CEO, about who a CEO is and what a CEO does. Because those ideas are so widespread, a good place to start is by dispelling some of them for the nonprofit sector—because this job is not what most people think.

Plenty of people may dream of being a CEO because they want the big salary and the glory that comes with it. If you're getting into nonprofit work, I say turn back now if that's where all of your drive is coming from. Though it might pay to be a ruthless CEO in some niches, that has never been what I'm about. All of my life experience has led me to imagine a new ideal for nonprofit leadership.

You have to be a compassionate CEO.

To organize and lead a successful nonprofit, you have to leave your ego at the door. You have to be mission-driven and your organization needs to be mission-based. You can't only rely on convenient connections to raise funds, and you can't think you're going to be off on vacation while your organization runs itself. Even if it looks like the highest position on the totem pole, the compassionate CEO knows he can't stand taller than anybody else.

If you're looking to be at the top in the nonprofit world, you need a big heart and you need resilience. You'll need to be a leader, a community organizer, a cheerleader, a fund-raiser and a shoulder to cry on. You need to have open ears, an open-door policy and damn near 24/7 availability to the people you're helping.

It's not for everybody. But then again, the non-profit world needs more compassionate CEOs.

Chapter 2:
Why Nonprofits Now?

A Brief History of Nonprofits

All the stereotypes about nonprofits had to start somewhere. Compared to for-profit businesses, nonprofit organizations—or 501(c)(3)s, if you want to be technical—are a relatively new phenomenon.

For-profit companies go all the way back to the beginnings of modern capitalism, and the idea is pretty simple: you and a group of people incorporate and you make a product or offer a service. You then sell that product or service, collect profit and reinvest it into your business (and most of the time, the owners and shareholders take most of the profits and the employees get salaries).

Though there are plenty of great businesses out there, whether or not they "do good" in their communities is sort of beyond their scope.

In other words, a company may *incidentally* do good or contribute to the community for some external reason, but that isn't why it exists. And even if it's clear to a small business what it would mean to do good locally, in the case of an international business, it's not always entirely clear what their "community" even is. To be in good ethical standing with the entire world is a pretty daunting prospect. Instead, a business's first priority is to create profit for their shareholders, period.

Nonprofits are different—sort of.

Though by definition, nonprofits *are* concerned with doing good in their communities, the successful ones really aren't that different from for-profit businesses when it comes to how they're organized. As I always say, running a nonprofit is really no different than running a business (at least it shouldn't be, if you're going to be successful).

The main difference between for-profit companies and 501(c)(3)s comes down to how they're taxed by the US government. To put it in roughly the same terms as Title 26 in the IRS tax code, a 501(c)(3) is a tax-exempt "corporation...community chest, fund, or foundation" whose primary purpose is essentially to do good. They are charities and social service organizations, and their profits don't go towards "the benefit of any private shareholder or individual."

That already seems pretty specific, but there are even more specific guidelines about what kinds of "good" causes are eligible for 501(c)(3) status. As the code says, these groups' purposes have to be *exclusively* dedicated to charitable, religious, scientific, literary, educational or public safety purposes. Even more specifically, the guidelines also apply to groups fostering national and international amateur sports (if that doesn't include the "provision of athletic facilities or equipment") and to preventing cruelty to animals or children.

When it comes to Children's Home, it is eligible on a number of those counts.

While it may seem noble that the IRS included a section in their tax code giving benefits to these organizations, the history of nonprofits is messier and more diffuse than that. Philanthropy and charity have obviously existed in America (and in the world) forever, but before the Revolutionary War, charity was mostly a small-scale social thing. Citizens might give money or food to their needy neighbors, and you might donate money to the church, but the disbursement of those funds was mostly local.

When the Revolutionary War came around, things changed.

All the men enlisted to fight and the women were left to hold the communities together. In addition to taking on more chores and work on the home front, they started organizing charities and other organizations that could serve as a kind of social glue.

The same was true during the Civil War.

Though there are plenty of examples in history, Children's Home is an excellent example of this pattern at work.

In essence, the history of the organization started in 1866 after a group of civically inclined women from Peoria got together to form the Christian Home Mission. What these women did was to divide the town up into sections and visit households to see who was struggling and needed relief.

In 1875, the Christian Home Mission got a charter from the state of Illinois and opened what was called a "Home for the Friendless," which originally had room for only six to eight children. Twenty years after that, they grew to have room for 60 women and children. By 1912, there were accommodations for 16 to 20 more girls. That organization grew and grew and was later renamed The Children's Home Association of Illinois.

But still, that's just one example.

Beyond women's involvement in the social sector, things took another turn in the Progressive Era, which ran from roughly the 1890s to the 1920s. At that time, activists thought rich industrialists and big business might be starting to pose a threat to direct democracy. Among a population of about 50 million in the 1870s, there were only 100 millionaires. By 1892, there were 4,047—and by 1916, there were 40,000.

Some of the biggest figures in the history of American industry made their names during that era—people like Andrew Carnegie and John D. Rockefeller. In 1901, Carnegie sold his company US Steel to JP Morgan for $480 million—the equivalent of $372 billion in

2014. Likewise, Rockefeller would be worth roughly $409 billion today according to his 1913 tax returns.

But one of the biggest developments in the formation of modern nonprofits was "The Gospel of Wealth," an article Carnegie wrote and published in 1889.

In his article, Carnegie argued it was the responsibility of the new upper class of rich Americans to launch a robust philanthropic industry. Though there's plenty to debate about Carnegie's ideas on how hard work and integrity *always* lead to wealth—and about who deserved charity and who didn't—his article is basically the foundation of the philosophy underlying modern American philanthropy.

Those ideas have also become part of the philosophy behind modern nonprofits.

Following those principles, Carnegie and Rockefeller used the wealth they'd amassed by the end of their lives to open massive philanthropic trusts and foundations. The Carnegie Foundation for the Advancement of Teaching was established in 1905 and The Rockefeller Foundation started in 1913.

Both organizations had the goal of doing social good as their main objective, and both developed a lot of close partnerships with other local businesses to do so. One of the first big projects The Rockefeller Foundation did, for example, was to give a $100,000 grant to the American Red Cross to buy a headquarters in Washington, D.C.

While plenty of other developments happened along the way, the main takeaway is that as these foundations sprung up, the US government was having a more difficult time regulating and dealing with them. Between 1913 and 1918, Congress passed many new laws to establish tax-exempt status for philanthropic organizations (and to regulate the taxes better). In 1918, the Revenue Act, which allows tax deductions for charitable donations, was passed. That gave wealthy citizens a financial incentive to donate their money.

The crown jewel of all these pieces of legislation was the Revenue Act of 1954, which established the modern tax code as we know it. It included Section 501(c), which outlines all the modern guidelines for operating a tax-exempt organization along with all the rules to stay in good standing.

Though there are 29 different ways to avoid getting federally taxed, it's mostly the third paragraph that applies directly to the kinds of organizations dedicated to the social good we're talking about (hence 501(c)(3)).

For our purposes, that's enough history.

After 1954, nonprofits started to operate and look like a lot of the nonprofits of today. Still, those old-school philanthropies like Carnegie and Rockefeller's were mostly funded through a single, enormous and private endowment. After that, they let the interest roll in and gave away just enough each year so that the core piggy bank would never run dry.

Though that kind of business thinking still exists and there's still some of those kinds of trusts around (those two certainly still are), the nonprofit industry has still changed considerably over the years. Carnegie and Rockefeller were two enormous fish in one giant pond.

Today, there are a lot more fish—and a lot more ponds, too.

The Post-Carnegie World

The point of explaining all of that is to say that a nonprofit usually starts with an end in mind. For Carnegie, it was education. For Rockefeller, it was "the well-being of humanity" (admittedly, that one's a little more general).

In both of those cases, there's an added benefit beyond the social good for the people doing it: it keeps the fortune in the family and preserves and reinvests money that's built up over a lifetime. Ever since Carnegie spoke about how the rich had a duty to spread or reinvest their wealth, Americans have been getting richer.

According to research by economists Emmanuel Saez and Gabriel Zucman, wealth concentration in America has gone up and down dramatically several times over the course of history. From the early 20th century until about 1929—right around the time we started seeing those mega-philanthropies from American industrialists—wealth inequality was stark. In 1929, 25 percent of American household wealth was held by 0.1 percent of the population.

That was the equivalent of about 160,000 people.

Still, things changed between about 1929 and 1978. While that initial re-injection of capital into the market in the late 1920s definitely redistributed wealth to the masses, there were plenty of other major economic shifts around that time as well.

The stock market crash and the Great Depression of 1929 were caused by wealth inequality, and the results were awful for everyone. Millions of investors lost their wealth, unemployment skyrocketed, money supply was low and plenty of people were unable to feed their families.

But the Great Compression that followed doesn't get talked about as much.

In part because of progressive policies like the New Deal and also because of the post-war policies following World War II, America was building up a rock-solid middle class.

The difference in wealth between the richest Americans and the poorest Americans was narrower than it had ever been before, and it seemed like things were going to be great once again. After a major "market correction," everything was back on track. It was a "compression" of wages, of the financial gap between Americans and an atmosphere of growth and stability where the whole country was on the rise again.

Unfortunately, that changed yet again right around 1978. To this day, the top and bottom sectors have been running in opposite directions when it comes to wealth.

As a matter of fact, we're now approaching Great Depression-levels of wealth inequality once again. Though the average standard of living might be better overall than it was in the 1920s (from advances in technology and medicine, for example), it still means that there are a lot of people out there who need some help.

While there's a lot of deep reading out there about all the connections between wealth and charity, one thing seems to be true above all. When there is serious wealth inequality, there are a lot of people who get left behind.

Fortunately, there's also a renewed interest and support for people and organizations that are willing to help those in need.

Ever since the IRS finalized their guidelines for tax-exempt organizations, it was clear that people wanted to start as many organizations and businesses in the 501(c)(3) category as possible. Many of them probably did so because they saw an opportunity to help people that also provided some personal benefits. There was probably plenty of others who saw it as a way to take advantage of the ability to form tax-exempt organizations in an emerging space.

Whatever the case, the nonprofit sector has grown into a pillar of the US economy since 1954. It's ballooned even more in more recent years, while growth in the for-profit sector has slowed.

According to a report published by the nonprofit recruiting firm PNP Staffing Group; the nonprofit sector has grown some 20 percent in the past 10 years. The for-profit sector, on the other hand, has only increased by about three percent in that same amount of time. This means a lot of things for people working in nonprofits, and one is that nonprofit hiring is up by about 50 percent.

The only problem is that the talent marketplace for nonprofits is shrinking.

There might be all kinds of reasons for that, but it's the state of nonprofits today. On the one hand, people all over the place are seeing just how much good nonprofits can achieve, how they can build up communities and make a difference in people's lives. On the other hand, while there may be a surge of people getting involved at all levels of the nonprofits sector, employee longevity is a concern. And part of that is simply because of how tough it is to work at a nonprofit.

When you get a job at an established for-profit company like Ford or Chevrolet, you might start in a lower technical position with pretty good benefits and a good salary. While you're there, you're learning how things are done on the micro-level. Theoretically, you'll stay in that position for a while, and then maybe you'll get promoted up to manager (of a bunch of people who used to do what you did).

Now, you're making more money and you have more benefits.

Presumably, you can continue this trajectory for your whole life, assuming you're doing a good job, your colleagues like you and the company you're working for doesn't go under. But even if it does, you've now established a pattern for yourself working in the for-profit industry that's transferable. If you were a manager of engineers at one company, with a little bit of research and some training, you could very well be a manager of engineers at a similar company.

This is where the nonprofit world behaves a little bit differently than the for-profit sector.

Because the best nonprofits have to run lean and mean, sometimes the entry-level salaries aren't as competitive as they are at for-profit companies looking for the same skills. If you've gone to school for many years to be a therapist and you're looking for a job, you could take a position at a for-profit hospital where the clients pay with private insurance. On the other hand, you could take a position at a community-oriented nonprofit helping people who don't have insurance and can't pay.

Which situation do you think most people are likely to go for?

In both of these cases, you're getting a job where you're helping people who need it—and that's great.

But in the second case, you could make the argument that you're helping people who need help *more* than the first, perhaps.

At the very least, you could argue you're helping a more immediate and invisible group of people. In that sense, the work is very important—after all, there will never be a shortage of people who want to be paid more at for-profit organizations, but there will be a shortage in the nonprofit sector.

Though here we're only talking about jobs that are "in the trenches" within nonprofit organizations, a similar issue extends to people in leadership and executive positions as well.

Because a good nonprofit has to run like a business, you need people in leadership positions who have business minds. They need to be able to "sell" the services the organization provides to the community—at fundraisers, to government bodies and to whoever else can keep the machine running.

The problem is that these all-star people are also being recruited by for-profit organizations.

Those for-profit companies can sometimes offer more money, more benefits and less stress for roughly the same responsibilities. When people talk about income inequality within nonprofit organizations, one piece of the problem has to do with offering enough money to the top business minds to keep them engaged and interested in nonprofit work.

There are plenty of factors that contribute to this inequality, but it's a hard problem to solve. And it's one of the defining problems in the nonprofit industry right now.

Because a nonprofit organization focuses on one localized community, it's not likely to undergo exponential growth. It's going to need people who care about the community and who want to make a life out of serving those people's needs and improving their lives. You can absolutely make a living doing that at all levels, but it will also take a toll on you.

If you work at Nike, during your normal work hours you care about making and selling great shoes.

When you go home, you unplug your phone, reconnect with your family, and you rest easy until work the next day. If you're working at a nonprofit like Children's Home Association of Illinois—whether you're an executive or a caseworker—that simply won't be the case.

When you're helping children and parents who are on their bottom dollar, people who don't have a place to live and who need all kinds of help, you can't just turn off when you get home. If you really care about the work, you won't be able to. If a person you're working with calls you after your normal work hours with an emergency, you're going to feel compelled to take that call.

Situations like that happen a lot. And your best and most effective efforts are often invisible to the broader community.

In a corporate leadership position, doing a bad job or slipping up in your efforts might mean a lower stock price or a failure to make a sale. In plenty of nonprofits like Children's Home, those slippages can mean more people end up on the street.

It can even mean people losing their lives.

It's interesting that nonprofits have an "unsexy" reputation compared to so-called big business. The idea behind being a high-powered executive is partially ego-fueled. You're going to make a lot of money, you're going to be the boss, working in a high-risk, high-stakes world.

In short—you're going to be living in the fast lane.

But honestly, it doesn't get much more high-risk or high-stakes than working in nonprofit leadership. While nonprofits are on the rise for all the right reasons, one problem that remains is how to communicate the reality of what we do—and to make it sound as sexy as possible.

The Future of Nonprofits

As the nonprofit sector grows, the need for good talent to run those organizations is going to grow as well—and it's only going to get harder and more competitive.

As I said, nonprofits and philanthropic organizations aren't just a couple big fish in a giant pond serving the whole country anymore. Instead, sometimes it's a lot of scrappy small fish swimming in really small ponds—and all of them are competing for the same food (or dollars, in this case) to keep running.

That's where the challenges for the future of this industry come into play.

While there's plenty to learn from for-profit businesses about how to recruit and manage talent, how to market services and make sales, there are also some lessons about what not to do. Plenty of companies that offer similar products or services are in competition with each other. Put plainly, Nike and Adidas are after a lot of the same dollars when they're selling shoes. And they both want the other to lose, on some level.

When it comes to nonprofits, a lot of that mentality can transfer over—though I don't think it has to.

While it's true that nonprofits ought to compete with each other and themselves to be the best they can be, I have a strong belief in the power of collaboration over competition. Because what we're trying to do is qualitatively different than what most for-profit businesses are trying to accomplish.

If you work in the nonprofit industry providing community services, over time you're going to see a lot of other organizations like yours springing up. Some of these businesses may be doing a great job spreading the word in the community and serving needs that aren't being served. On the other hand, some non-profits are less efficiently run, offering duplicated services or programs that are being done better by other organizations.

It's in those situations that the nonprofit sector has a potential advantage over for-profit organizations.

If you're thinking of it in a Darwinian sense, you might be thinking that the "weaker" organizations just have to die out and the bigger fish need to absorb the money and resources they've been taking from the community. The problem with that, though, is that those smaller fish are actually organized groups of people who are already trying to do a thankless job and trying to help—and that's a huge resource in itself!

It's important in those cases not to focus so much on direct competition, but on collaboration and communication. The goal of both organizations in this hypothetical situation is to raise money, keep as many people paid as possible and to provide great programs and services to the community.

By getting in touch with one another, learning about what's working and what's not, there can be growth and reorganization so that everybody can still help in a better way. Above all, leadership teams don't want to get caught in the mentality that if one organization in the space "wins," the other organizations "lose."

That's stupid thinking.

Beyond the more technical challenges of managing and recruiting, there's another huge element of maintaining a healthy nonprofit sector that needs addressing. That element is storytelling, and it's going to come up again and again.

As I said, nonprofits don't have the sexiest reputation. But some of it is because of the way we talk about what we do.

When somebody asks me what I do, I don't tell them, "I run an organization that provides mental health services, residential services, education and other wraparound services to homeless youth and families." That may be accurate on the surface, but it's not true to the *heart* of what I do that people really care about.

Instead, I'm going to say, "At Children's Home we change lives and save lives."

When it comes to nonprofits, we have a complicated PR problem that looks different from all sides.

From an older generation's perspective, there's sometimes a harmful stereotype that somehow nonprofits aren't "real businesses," and you'll have people condescending to you for that.

From a middle-aged perspective, you have people appreciating what you do and thinking of you as a business with some integrity, but maybe they just aren't excited about it. Maybe they think they can make more money somewhere else, or that the effort they put into your organization isn't going to pay off (at least in the sense that it's worth taking less money up front to do it).

Finally, from a younger perspective, you have people who are willing to help and willing to offer their time—but they're looking at your organization skeptically. How do they know that your nonprofit is efficiently and ethically run? If they're just starting their career, how do they know that they ought to start it with you? How do they know that their efforts are going to make a difference?

All the scenarios above have different angles and different concerns, but they come down to *storytelling* and *outcomes*.

As some people might've gleaned from my experiences fundraising and doing events with my cousin, a big part of nonprofit sales happens through social networking. Still, in some ways that was truer in the past than it is today. The reputation that nonprofits developed in the past as a way that the rich could avoid taxes, maintain their wealth and have a social club is not entirely untrue—at least, it wasn't once upon a time.

Things are different today. These days there are many more people competing for the same money, so it takes a lot more to keep an organization alive than just knowing so-and-so who runs some big business in town. Everybody has their hand out for corporate dollars and sponsorships now.

As a result, that big local businessman has 100 other people knocking down his door asking for the same money you want.

The best way to get funding today is by telling a powerful story and offering a compelling vision for your community. Our story is that we're a large agency in Illinois offering best-in-class services for what we do. We're interested in saving lives and changing lives, and we're not afraid to do whatever it takes to accomplish that.

With that part in place, you're going to need to have data to prove how good your organization's outcomes are. It's one thing to tell people a pretty story about what you're doing, but it's another thing to show them exactly how you're doing it. When you're able to connect to donors' hearts in a personal way, to show them why what you're doing matters, you're halfway there.

When you can show donors exactly how their money will make a difference—and how it already is working—that's even better. Though there's no telling which nonprofits will be around or what new ways they'll be able to help in 10 years, these two elements aren't going anywhere.

Chapter 3:
The Big Picture
Behind Nonprofits

How Nonprofits Operate

It was easy in the past to write off nonprofits as charities or non-businesses, and we know today that's just not true (especially in a world where nonprofits are so much more competitive). Still, it's not enough to say that nonprofits are just like businesses.

It's important to understand how a nonprofit actually works from start to finish. So, let's start there.

For any social service agency, everything begins with the mission. Before you hire people, start offering programs or "investing in community," you need a clear idea of what your vision is and what you'll offer. The mission of an agency is going to dictate its programs and approach to those programs.

When you look at what a social service agency does, the mission will decide how the funding is dictated.

In the case of The Children's Home Association of Illinois, it's a 30-million-dollar agency that has 50 plus different programs funded by many different grants and revenue streams. It works with United Way, the Department of Children and Family Services, the Department of Human Services, the Department of Health, the Illinois State Board of Education, the Department of Juvenile Justice, the local city and the state.

Our mission is giving children a childhood and a future. My personal mission is changing lives and saving lives—for children and families from Peoria and from all over the great state of Illinois.

To that end, The Children's Home Association's programs reflect this mission by taking a multi-faceted approach to behavioral and mental health. Our services include behavioral health, residential services, foster care and other supports for children and families. Because we're such a large organization, our roster of services may be broader than some other nonprofits—but you can trace each one of our programs back to our mission.

We don't want people to think of Children's Home as just foster care. We also don't want anybody thinking that we only offer housing. The truth is that what we do depends on the child in question. Our approach is highly individualized and all-encompassing. The way we operate is really no different than a major business with different product lines that are all vertically integrated. We're a one-stop shop.

While we take a complex approach to serious problems, you could just as easily have a nonprofit with a complex approach to a not-so-serious problem.

There are plenty of other nonprofits that are one-stop shops just like we are—think of the YMCA, for example. The YMCA's mission is to provide community-centered services that help people build strength in mind, body and spirit. The YMCA is also a Christian organization, so that plays a role as well. Though they have a worthy mission, what they do is largely about fitness and recreation and community.

This isn't to downplay the good work that the YMCA does; behavioral health just isn't their focus.

Regardless, there's no way to argue that the YMCA isn't a complex organization. It has 1,000s of locations and each one has fitness programs, outreach programs, weights and fitness areas. Most of them even have public pools. Within their niche, they have their specialties and their strengths.

Given those details, it would be hard for them to stray from their core strengths and expand into other areas.

It would be next to impossible for the YMCA to expand into foster care, for example—that's not their area of expertise. To keep their organization running smoothly, they're not going to stretch their services into areas that other organizations are already doing well.

' Instead, they're going to dig down into their focus areas and go after funding tied to the things at which they already excel.

To bring the point back to Children's Home, we have a high-needs school and a school for kids with autism. Because schooling is a key factor in the overall picture of helping homeless youth, it applies to our mission and so we're involved in that area.

Still, it's a part of our organization that adds a lot of complexity.

No matter where you are, school districts are typically paid and regulated by the state. In our case, Illinois's Board of Education defines a rate that they'll pay from the budget for a statewide educational focus area.

At our school or our Academy for Autism, our operating budget comes partially from the state, and partially from other grants and funds. In these programs and others like them, some are funded federally, some locally and others are funded statewide. In many cases, it's a combination of all three.

Things can get tricky, however, when it comes to results and documentation.

As a hypothetical, a social service agency may be running a million-dollar program where $600,000 is coming from a state or federal entity, $200,000 is coming from a private grant and $200,000 is coming from United Way.

It's great to have those three different and diverse funding streams that let you run your programs. But you now also have three different sets of reports due quarterly to each of those partners or funding streams, and each one has their own requirements about exactly how their money gets spent.

Clearly, this can get complicated very fast—but that's just the nature of the business.

Even if it means more paperwork, having more funding streams is better than having fewer. A problem that many smaller nonprofits run into is that their funding sources are not very diverse. They may only have a few income streams coming in that they rely on to stay operational.

Let's imagine, for example, that there's a small nonprofit offering senior services that gets its money from the state. Let's then say that the state budget cuts some of its allotment for senior services and all the programs running off that money are now underfunded by about 30 percent.

If that organization can't find a creative way to adapt, that state budget loss will get passed down directly. It means that nonprofit will lose 30 percent of its business (or cut 30 percent of its services).

If you compared what Children's Home did to an all-encompassing for-profit agency, that agency would basically run no differently than a doctor's office. They would offer their specific set of services; they would have certain facilities and rates that they set themselves (within the boundaries of any applicable state guidelines). But ultimately, they would be taking in people who had money and they could charge whatever they wanted.

Children's Home provides very similar types of services in a comprehensive way. But we do it for free, at no cost to the people using them. We are able to accomplish this through our use of strategic community building, business partnerships and state partnerships.

And we've been doing it that way for more than 153 years.

An Investment in Community

When it comes to gathering funding for a non-profit, I always say that an investment in an organization like Children's Home is an investment in community. But it's not always clear exactly what that means.

Let me paint a broad picture.

Let's say there are 100 homeless people on the streets in a town, and there's an organization that offers a homeless program for those people. Let's say the program takes them in, gives them a place to live and provides them with support to get back on their feet. They get emotional and psychological help, they get some job training, and they have their self-worth back.

When all is said and done, those 100 people are then integrated back into society as productive, tax-paying citizens. From the individual standpoint, that organization has done well by 100 people who were at their lowest point when they came in. It has taken 100 people who had essentially been forgotten and turned them into functioning members of society with all the tools to succeed.

That's certainly a positive result, but it's not the only one.

From a business standpoint, the town now has 100 more potential employees available for hire. They have more people that can pay taxes to fund community programs and services. While this makes complete sense on paper, people sometimes have a problem connecting all the dots. Nobody wants to intervene or to pay an upfront cost to turn around a bad outcome in the present—but when you look at the future and the alternative of doing nothing, it makes so much sense.

Having a functional nonprofit that helps at-risk kids or families is a benefit to the community in a very real—and not in abstract or moralizing—way. While you *can* look at it from a mission-based standpoint and say yes, this is ethically the right thing to do, there's still a lot more to it than that.

It also makes sense from a financial perspective when you look at the numbers more closely and critically.

If a situation where children are getting into trouble in the streets goes unchecked, the truth is that they're still "investing" in a kind of community—it's just a community that you don't particularly want to see grow. Those kids are still spending time with one another, still forging relationships in a negative context—one that encourages behavior that will potentially deteriorate and dissolve the wider and more positive community beyond the one they're forming.

When people refuse to help in situations like this, the problems progress and get worse. In some cases, it leads to those kids going to jail—and while that's bad from an ethical perspective, it's also bad from a financial perspective.

Consider the cost of running a small community program versus the cost of keeping a substantial number of kids in jail year after year. Ultimately, a community is going to pay those costs somewhere no matter what. From my perspective, it makes more sense to pay them proactively in a way that builds community rather than paying them later when it's too late.

When it comes to Children's Home and to other nonprofits like us, it doesn't make sense to talk about "us" and "the community" as if they were separate things. In truth, we are the community and the community is us.

All told, we have 450 employees who work in town or nearby. Children's Home is one of the top 15 employers in Peoria. When you consider the fact that the other big employers in the area are Fortune 500 companies, hospitals and schools, that's a fact we're very proud of. At any rate, those 450 employees are paying taxes, living in the area, supporting other small businesses and so on—everything a town wants.

On the one hand, investing in a nonprofit like Children's Home means investing in services for the people who need help, sure. But what often goes overlooked is the fact that investing in Children's Home also helps the people who work at Children's Home, the vast majority of whom have long-standing roots in the community already.

Whenever someone asks me a question about what a nonprofit organization is doing, or whether the money they're spending is worth it, I encourage them to try to see the value that may seem invisible at first. I always ask: What would happen if we *didn't* do what we're doing? What if there were no community-based programs? How many more kids would be on the streets? How many kids would end up in jail or trafficked?

Without a doubt, these kinds of programs change and save lives—that's proven—and anybody who signs up on that promise is going to get what they paid for. But the results are also a huge deterrent against social stagnation and deterioration that benefits everybody. Those benefits extend to the business community, to anybody passing through town and to private tax-paying citizens who may think these problems don't concern them.

The solutions that good nonprofits like Children's Home provide help transform communities for the better. Because if you don't have programs that help kids stay out of jail, that help reunite families, you end up getting an even more fractured state of affairs than already exists.

And that's a situation that benefits nobody.

Once you accept the premise that a nonprofit represents an investment in community, you can start to ask how that manifests in different ways. How does that investment start to pay dividends to its investors? Aside from the above, there's a lot of other ways to answer that question.

The money that flows through a good nonprofit helps the people in the community who work there, and it also helps the people in the community the organization is there to serve. But what I'd also like to suggest is profound in its implications, even if it seems simple:

The more you invest in people, the more valuable they become.

Though every life obviously has value all on its own, we can think about this idea in a strictly pragmatic sense. If a kid is in jail, for example, what are they going to accomplish either for themselves or for their community—particularly if they enter the penal system when they're still very young?

Those are the kinds of cost that a community pays for a lifetime—for generations, even.

As the CEO of Children's Home, part of my responsibility is to spread the story of our team and services. Another part of it is to build the brand of Children's Home, to be a cheerleader and to attract good board members and donors. But even beyond that, I have the job of protecting the agency as a whole. I can't let people pierce the veil of our agency, so to speak. And the veil is the esteem, the longevity and the good reputation of Children's Home.

To that end, I have an obligation to deliver the best outcomes possible where the quality and the fidelity can never drop—that's a given. But it also means I have to protect my employees and their families as well. Since so many different people pass through Children's Home's' doors, those people also become a part of its legacy. With that being the case, I need to be sure everyone who comes through is treated in the best way possible.

Though I'm just one piece of a very large organization, it's my job to go out into the world and talk about it in a very confident way—and any nonprofit CEO ought to do the same. We have to talk to donors and supporters as if they were our investors in a very real way. Because though they're definitely investing in you, they're also investing in your agency, employees and the larger community.

No matter what, you have to get people to invest.

Nonprofits Are Like Stocks

While it's good to get money from all kinds of different sources, you better be providing a good product for whatever money you accept. Sustainability is a big issue for nonprofits that extends from fundraising, and it's a place where organizations have to prove themselves again and again every year.

Whether you're a nonprofit or a for-profit business, you have to produce results when people invest. But with a nonprofit, it is essential to not only provide the services you say you will, but also the *quality*.

The quality is the fidelity of the program and how well the program is actually living up to its mission. It's the ethical piece of the program. When it comes to getting funding for nonprofit programs individually, it makes a lot of sense to think about nonprofits like stocks—even if that seems a little counter-intuitive.

To understand what that means, it's important to think about what nonprofits were like 10 years ago versus what they're like today. If you go back a decade, it was easier to get funding through personal and business relationships—especially by going through foundations. If you had someone on your nonprofit board that was part of a department or foundation with money to give away, you could have that person make a request.

Maybe you would get the money you asked for, maybe you wouldn't, or maybe you'd land somewhere in between. Today, funding is much more driven by mission and focus areas. Though relationships are still important, it's ultimately the tangible *outcomes* that are most important. Good outcomes drive funding. And if you don't have good outcomes, your funding will dry up.

Nonprofits often struggle because they don't have the wherewithal or the community support to back up their mission—or their dollars. They're not delivering the results they promise to deliver.

When I say that nonprofit programs are like stocks, I mean that "investors"—your community members, business leaders, foundations, government bodies, whoever it is—are going to be looking closely at the return on investment when it comes time to "buy" or "sell." Just like regular stocks, someone may initially buy in because they heard good things on television about the company, or they have an investor friend who gave them a tip that the company was worth looking at.

But the problem is that sometimes a stock's listed price doesn't always accurately reflect its value—a stock can be over or under-valued at different times.

For a standard stock, the most basic metric to see what it's worth is the price-to-earnings ratio. To calculate that, you would take the stock's price and divide it by the earnings you stand to make per share. Typically speaking, the lower the ratio, the faster you make back the money that you invested. Still, serious investors will look at all other kinds of metrics and figures to determine the health of a stock. The same thing is true for nonprofit programs.

When you're taking money from any outside source, you have to be prepared for other people to look into the details of your business. For that reason, it's important to not only have great outcomes but also great relationships. You also need an excellent board, good communication within the company and a solid presence within the community.

All of those factors go into building a great brand, which is the public face your community will see.

Beyond that, it's also important to maintain that brand by being transparent with your investors. If you're struggling in a certain area of your services, you have to be very clear and honest. Explain that there's an aspect of your business that needs improvement—but that you're excelling in other ways (after all, you want to keep their confidence up).

When it comes to Children's Home, I take great pride in running it as an ethical business. I have open communication with my board, and I don't hide a thing, good or bad. After all, something good or bad is bound to happen every five minutes. I know our testimonials are real, and they are life and death. If you peel back my head, I might have 1,000 stories. Five hundred might be good and 500 might be bad, but they're all true—and that's the difference between a transparent business and an opaque or deceptive one.

If I tell the story about a kid whose parents were murdered, a kid who went in the system and needs help but now has a chance, that's a compelling story. But it's still just one story. What good visionaries and good marketing people can do is weave the right stories in the right circumstances. Part of being a good leader is walking into a crowd, reading them and knowing which story you want to tell.

But at the end of the day, none of the stories are lies.

The fun part of my job is being able to tell stories that knock reality into people so they understand what's happening around them. It's not to make them feel bad or guilty to force them to write a check. It's to make them understand what we do. If they end up writing a check, that's fine—but it's a lot bigger than that. It affects everyone.

There's even a difference between investing in specific programs and investing in a broader organization like Children's Home as a whole. Though I typically don't talk about it this way, investing in a nonprofit like Children's Home is more like investing in a mutual fund than an individual stock. Because there's no telling how that initial investment you made is going to be used on our end. And you don't know where the majority of your "profit" is going to come out on the other end.

There may be a homeless person we help who becomes rich and successful and wants to give back, and now he's helping a donor's child who's struggling with drugs. Or maybe a donor was a foster child in the system growing up, or maybe he lost his family in a tragic accident when he was younger. Whatever it is, the work Children's Home does touches on some aspect of each of those stories.

In that way, nonprofits are like a mutual fund. A community dividend can come out of one program or out of many programs. But no matter what, all of the benefits go directly back into the community.

At the end of it all, what remains is a question for potential investors: Would you rather invest in an agency with great outcomes, a solid board, great presence, good relationships with funders and great community leaders? Or would you invest in an agency where funding has been cut, they're struggling, not open to collaboration, and everyone's egos are involved?

Where are you going to invest?

Chapter 4:
Running a Big Business

Running a $30 Million Dollar Nonprofit

There are thousands of nonprofits across the United States, all with their own clearly defined missions and purposes. Still, one thing that's a little less clear is a sense of scale when it comes to running a nonprofit as a business. If you live in a small town, the local church qualifies as a nonprofit. For the most part, a church's purpose is to provide religious or moral instruction to the town members.

They might hold free church services a few times a week, for example. They might have a few employees on hand, do collections periodically and even do charity drives for the local community. All of this is good work, and a church in a small town is likely a pillar of the community.

Still, running a small church in a town of a few thousand people is completely different than running a nonprofit like Children's Home. One is a small church; the other is a $30 million-dollar business.

To break it down, it helps to get a picture of what our organization looks like—that way, people understand that it's not just "an orphanage." Children's Home has many different locations offering various services all around Peoria.

There's a main campus that houses all the administrative staff along with our foster care programs, intact family programs and youth services programs. Beyond that, there's an academy campus that's home to our school for children with autism and the offices of our supervised independent living programs.

There's a separate building that houses all the offices for our behavioral health programs and another building for Good Beginnings—that's our program for first-time moms and children up to three years old. At that campus, we can link up new moms with doula services, early childhood programs and teen parent programs as well.

After that, there's Scott's Prairie, a 76-acre farm that our kids can use for all kinds of activities and recreation. Above all, it's a place for our kids to learn job skills, enjoy nature and experience a kind of sanctuary to get away from the other stresses of life. We also offer behavioral health services and crisis teams. Lastly, there's our Youth Farm campus, a residential treatment program for boys and girls between the ages of 12 and 18.

Through all those different locations and programs, we help more than 1,700 children a month—

though when you consider the extended network around those kids, it's likely we're helping even more people than that. To run that whole organization and to take care of all those kids requires a lot—around 450 people, 50-plus programs and 30 million dollars. And we're one of the largest social service agencies of our kind in downstate Illinois.

Because the organization is so expansive, there are lessons to learn from Children's Home about how to do good on a big, scalable level. We have built an organization that can address a community of a couple hundred thousand people.

To that end, we are a big business and we run as a big business.

As I previously stated, CEO role means being a cheerleader for the Children's Home brand. But I also need to be a brand in myself. After all, our community is facing a crisis and I need to bust down doors with a smile on my face and speak positively about it all the time.

Working right by my side, our President and CFO needs to make strategic decisions and manage all the financial complexity of the organization. After that, the board helps guide our decision-making as a handful of brilliant community leaders and business minds that offer their time—for free—and ideas on how we can do better.

To stay in touch with the community and to keep the brand visible, we have our Development team. On the other side of that are donors and supporters in the community and at the level of local government. I try to never call them donors. Whenever possible, I call them our champions. Without their support and their willingness to get behind our mission, we wouldn't be able to help as many children and families. And usually, they don't just decide to help us one time—these folks often pledge their support continually.

After that, is the frontline staff—that's our social workers, clinicians and our team that works directly with the kids. "Frontline" refers to all the people who work directly with the kids and families we serve. I often say that these people are the lifeblood of our organization. They're the ones who bear some of the greatest emotional tolls, and they're the ones who make sure they're always available to help however they can.

They put themselves and their families on the line to do good for others. As such, it's my job to completely have their back, to watch out for them and to ensure that their own mental health is taken care of as well. Looking at Children's Home as a business, the frontline staff and the services are the "product" that we provide—the other parts are marketing, sales, administrative departments, facilities, IT and so on.

Finally, the last major piece of the organization are the kids and families we serve—they are the people we've been tasked to care for, and they're our "customers" in a sense. They're the entire reason we exist and without them, we wouldn't even have a business. Still, it's impossible to say what element of our business is "most important," or which level leads the rest.

We work together, and we all follow and support each other.

When you look at that closely, it's clear how much of a business a nonprofit like Children's Home really is, even if we are "mission-based." Part of the stigma that the nonprofit sector faces is actually related to that divide. People consider us "noble people" or kindhearted, well-meaning do-gooders.

It's a mentality of pity, an attitude where people look at us, shake their heads and say, "I don't know how you do it." That's not what anybody in our business wants from the community. It's easy to see how and why we do it—we do it to better people's lives, to help families and whatever other groups can benefit from our services.

What gets hard in our business is that there are plenty of other great professions tied to heroism. The American public has a great relationship with the fire department, police, the military and so on. We love all the people who put their lives on the line in those professions, and we should—all of those people make great sacrifices and are heroes.

But as a CEO, it's important for me to stand up for all the people I work with and to campaign for them as heroes as well. That's particularly true of our front-line staff, but it's also true of everybody else who helps these children and families. Our social service teams are absolutely at the same level of heroism as police and firefighters. They save lives and they ensure a better future for our communities. They're the compassionate heart of everything.

It's an important piece that doesn't get talked about enough.

Whenever someone asks me, "What would happen if there wasn't a Children's Home?" I have to tell them, "You don't want to know." In our line of work, we see kids who are still going to school who haven't eaten for 24 to 48 hours. There are kids missing school because they're couch surfing or they're between places. Some are kids who've lost everything and are on the street because their parents died.

The bottom line is there's a lot of fight in the people who pass through the doors of Children's Home — kids and staff alike. And many don't understand the grit and the fire in the bellies of people who want to make things better.

So, running a big nonprofit like Children's Home requires sales, organization, communication and synergy — just like any great business. And like any great business, it also requires a great product.

The only difference is our product is people, and the quality can't slip whatsoever.

Risk and Rewards

Though it's easy to understand how much social service nonprofits look just like businesses and why they should be run that way, there's a deeper question about *why* that gets left unsaid. In other words, *why* organize yourself as a nonprofit in the first place rather than a for-profit business that provides a bunch of the same services?

After all, there are definitely plenty of for-profit businesses out there with great services helping their communities, right?

The point of asking this is not to argue that everyone should offer services for free—far from it. It's just to show that there are risks and rewards that come with any way of organizing a business.

As a 501(c)(3), there are some pretty obvious risks that jump out from the very beginning. For one thing, you'll need to make sure you're following all the necessary guidelines to actually be a nonprofit organization, and you must run your organization transparently and ethically to stay that way. You also need to have a solid foundation from top to bottom to be able to grow in such a competitive market.

In the past five to 10 years, there's been a huge explosion of growth in the nonprofit sector. Whenever a new nonprofit develops, whether it's a program, a charity or a social service agency with funding tied to it, there are now more fish eating from the same pond.

When it comes to keeping nonprofits afloat, the bigger the agency you want to be, the more diverse you have to be when it comes to funding.

If you're a for-profit business, on the other hand, you can manage your budget and your profits in a lot of ways. You can sell fewer things for a higher price. You can lay people off. You can pare down your business in whatever way makes the profits higher than the expenses. The fact of the matter is a lot of those options aren't really options if you're running an ethical nonprofit whose goal is to take care of its community.

For one thing, you can't sell your free product for a higher price—free is free.

For another, you can't think you'll just lay people off if you run out of money, either—the people who work for you are more than just employees, they're community members and they're basically your family. My Dad always said as a CEO, you're not just in charge of 450 people, you're also charged with taking care of their families. And that's a responsibility I respect and love.

Finally, paring down your business doesn't mean quite the same thing when you're not selling consumer goods. At a social service agency, cutting programs might mean cutting important services that people in need are desperately relying on.

And any nonprofit that needs help can't go around slashing programs and services to save a quick buck.

Still, it's a real risk that growing nonprofits could have too few funding streams or be too reliant on government and local grants. At any time, budgets and policies can change and funding can get cut or adjusted. What happens then?

An important point to make here is that there's a bit of a difference between your funding streams on paper and your actual cash flow.

Typically, social service agencies have operational programs that have been running for long periods of time. A lot of money gets put into a program and it grows from a service standpoint, but much of the time it's not growing internally from an infrastructure standpoint. For instance, maybe the funding of a program stays the same along with its outcomes and expectations, but other parts of the program are becoming more expensive.

Maybe the personnel needs, technological needs or reporting needs have changed. And now you need more money. To avoid these issues, programs need to be audited internally all the time so that surprises like that don't pop up. But just to be prepared for when those situations inevitably do arise, it's good to have a reserve of free cash on hand.

Cash allows an agency to do many things. The obvious thing it does is help you meet your obligations—namely, dole out payroll and benefits. But you also need to have cash on hand so that you can grow as a business. Just like a for-profit organization, you need cash to expand. Even if you're not acquiring a new program, you need it to meet the needs of your ever-changing climate and community.

Any type of expansion, merger or acquisition requires capital, and having it means you can stay flexible. That flexibility can make you more stable in the long run and it can provide better outcomes for your programs. Beyond using your cash from a position of strength, however, you can also use it as a defense or a patch during hard times.

Occasionally, the hard times for your business are out of your control—when a state or federal budget gets slashed, for example, and it affects your services. In those situations, cash flow can buy you some time. Rather than shuttering programs and services, you use your cash to float you until you can find a longer-term solution.

To run a social service organization, it's vital to constantly be out in the community raising funds and juggling many balls at once to stay solvent (and to grow). And you also have to run your books well internally, anticipating any disasters that could be coming your way.

On that level, it's all a big competition for the same dollars. But on another level, it's a competition for the same people as well.

You want the absolute best people working for your organization no matter who you are, and this is an important distinction to make. Nonprofits aren't just competing with other nonprofits for talent, they're competing with colleges, hospitals and so on. It's a tough problem because in general, people—both civilians and those applying for entry-level jobs—don't seem to know what nonprofits are really about.

The people who typically get into this business for the long haul are mission-oriented and service-oriented 90 percent of the time. Typically, the other 10 percent or so like the idea of helping out on the surface but then get into the weeds and realize it's not for them—and that's not a bad thing, either. After all, not everyone that works at a social service agency does exactly the same thing and there are many ways to help.

I want people who are willing to go all in, all the time—especially when it comes to clinical and front-line staff.

From the business point-of-view, you have to sell your employees in a few different ways that make your agency more attractive than others in the space (or more attractive than for-profit agencies that have more money to offer).

In the case of Children's Home, we have a strategy we've developed for recruiting and hiring.

First, we emphasize that we are best in class when it comes to outcomes. Second, we're rock solid on our financials—we know how to budget, we know how to fundraise, and we know how to market and position ourselves. Finally, we mention how strong and giving our board is. But most importantly, it's about the kids.

Though it's the part of a nonprofit that often gets a bad reputation, a good board is a huge selling point on almost every level. In essence, when you're trying to woo a new employee, you can't just say, "Come work for us, we'll pay you this much," like you could at a for-profit. But you also can't just say, "Come work for us, we're about the mission."

You have to take a middle road, and you have to ask a lot of questions of your potential employees early on.

You need to ask probing questions about what a person is really looking for. Ideally, you're looking to hire people who are going to stay for at least three to five years. Although that doesn't sound like a very long time, in today's job market it is. Often, big social service agencies are lucky to get someone to stay for two to four years!

On the other side of things, you need to ask the kind of questions that elaborate on a person's character. In a lot of businesses, employees are looking for a good "work-life balance." And the bottom line is it's very hard to have that in this business. Working in the trenches of social service is no different than being an oncologist, a nurse or a teacher.

By way of example, my wife is a teacher. And she doesn't just come home and turn off. If she ever sees a kid come into school with an injury that wasn't there before, she doesn't just forget about it when the bell rings—and you shouldn't forget about it, either.

You can turn it off when you're selling tennis shoes, but not when people's lives are on the line.

The biggest risk of all is that the lives of the people you're supposed to protect are quite literally in your hands. From top to bottom, your team is responsible for delivering good outcomes in situations that sometimes seem nearly impossible. But because you've stepped in to help, you're now responsible. Communication and synergy among all levels are so important in a social service agency because if too many people drop the ball, people can get hurt.

Though there's probably more to list, those are some of the risks. But there are definitely rewards to reap, too.

The most significant one is that you're a tax-exempt organization. Though your accounting is still going to be complex, it'll be different than a for-profit business. And in a great social service agency, you want as much of it to go directly into the programs as possible while keeping your employees happy—and that's a fine line to balance.

Beyond that, you'll still have the chance to build fulfilling relationships with business and community leaders. In fact, the work that you do will be part of the bedrock of your community going into the future.

Raising money from different revenue streams could be a risk, but it can also be a reward. Although it works differently from nonprofit to nonprofit, most will be eligible for public and private grants that can help expand their programs.

Above all, the reward of working in social service and nonprofits that outweighs the risks is the direct good you can do for your community. You'll learn exactly what's going on in the community around you and you'll feel connected to and responsible for it. Even better than that, you will have put your efforts into making a difference in the worst situations imaginable, ensuring a better future.

Though there are risks to any venture, the nonprofit and social service sector has some of the highest stakes—but the rewards are sweet.

What It Takes

What it takes to run a successful agency is a hard question to answer. It's all the things that have been mentioned, but it's also even more specific.

Using Children's Home as an example, we can take it all the way down to a single case-level.

When people come through our doors, every situation and diagnosis is different. No two people will be alike and thus no two treatment plans will be exactly alike. Things usually begin with children being evaluated by one of our clinicians.

That interview will determine what the child has already been through. In some cases, maybe the kid is high functioning but there's some kind of abuse involved in the past and they need a certain protocol to deal with it. In other cases, you may be dealing with someone who lost their parents and needs help with depression and housing. No matter what the scenario is, our team takes detailed notes in that first stage.

After that, we assemble a special team for each case that can deal with different aspects of that child's situation. If you have children who are on any type of medication, you need protocols in place to supervise those regimens—that means coordinating with RNs, psychologists and psychiatrists.

While it's important to have all kinds of clear systems and protocols in place, it's also important to make sure that you have good leadership within all levels of your organization. While it's easy to think of the "bosses" as the people who are on the executive level, there's also a need for each department to run efficiently on its own while remaining in communication with the rest of the company.

If you're a one-stop-shop, your funding and your personnel really dictate how much good you can do.

And a lot of it comes down to your team.

Chapter 5:
The Nonprofit Team

The Staff

Now that we've looked at each of the different parts of a nonprofit organization, it pays to explore each one of them individually. After all, there's a lot more that goes into your typical nonprofit than meets the eye.

The parts of the organization that most people probably think of first are the frontline or clinical staff, though at Children's Home we never call them that.

We call them the team, and they're the lifeblood of what we do.

At Children's Home, the clinical staff is a key piece of the entire enterprise—they're the RNs, the social workers, the therapists and so on. But not all social service agencies have a clinical staff like we do. For example, consider Big Brothers Big Sisters of America.

Like us, they're a nonprofit trying to make a difference in children's lives. The difference is they do it by having adult mentors pair up with kids to help guide them. At that organization, the mentors would be the key part of the whole thing. At another organization, maybe it would be the core marketing team driving everything. But no matter what your mission or what you're doing, the structure and the idea behind it should be the same.

At the team level of your organization, everybody should have their own specific role to play and their unique responsibilities. In the case of Children's Home, all of our team members have a part to play in each child's stabilization and recovery.

But there's even more to our team than just the clinical people.

As it turns out, the cooks are just as important to our organization as the CEO. If it's all about helping kids and making them happy, nobody does a better job of putting smiles on kids' faces than our kitchen team. Beyond that, the maintenance team is also a huge part of what we do—keeping our facilities orderly and clean is a basic requirement before we can do anything else.

For those jobs and everybody in between, we try to hire people who aren't just there for the mission. We want people who are going to be there for *each other* as well. Working in social services is a very hard job, and we hope it becomes a career. With that mentality, the struggles the team deals with are the same ones the people around them have faced. They need to be able to lean on each other to get through it, or there's no way for them to succeed.

A common misconception about social service agencies and nonprofits is that the same type of strict power hierarchy defines what people do like at a for-profit company. Though there are different roles and positions at Children's Home, there's also fluidity among all levels of our organization.

Even though I'm the CEO, I go to all the new employee orientations. I'm always making site visits, checking in with employees and shaking hands with everybody I can.

I even make it my goal to learn every kid's name—and that's a nearly impossible goal. But it illustrates my point. Everybody we hire is there to further our mission, and therefore everybody in the organization is equally important. The only difference is that some people need to be completely focused on the kids, and others need to be focused on running the company.

And that's where the executive team comes in.

The Executive Team

If you were thinking of a nonprofit structure as a kind of pyramid, you might see the executive team as the middle layer between "the team" and the board.

In truth, the executives serve as the company's hands-on leadership team. At Children's Home, there are currently nine people on staff who take on the most responsibility and help guide the company. For us, that's the CEO, the President and CFO, the EVP in charge of clinical services and a whole group of Vice Presidents. We have Vice Presidents of IT and Facilities, Behavioral Health, Education, Foster Care, Residential and Independent Living and Human Resources. Under those nine or so people, we have directors and management. Below them are the coordinators and the clinical and frontline staff.

Though it's clear what the CEO and President and CFO are doing, the other Vice Presidents are all hugely important when it comes to running the organization smoothly. Because the clinical team has the most direct time with the kids, it's important to be in close communication with them (even about individual cases).

For that purpose, the VPs are indispensable.

Although they also likely have some experience in the areas they're overseeing, they're the ones who can assist the clinical team in making sure that they're delivering the best outcomes. When you have a staff as big as Children's Home's, the buck stops at the executive level.

Because of that, it's a lot of pressure and a lot of responsibility.

To keep your organization running smoothly, the executive team has to have meetings to get on the same page about outcomes, problems, census issues, inconsistencies and finances tied to each revenue stream. While all of that is important to go over together, maybe the most important things to focus on in executive meetings are the areas of risk.

When we're talking about risks, it can mean all kinds of things. It could be an internal risk that involves the kids we serve. It could mean there's a youth we're taking care of who is highly acute and needs more of our resources as we shuffle some things around. In crisis cases like this, the executive team needs to have a swift and unified response.

But the executives also manage business risk. It could mean there's a new business coming into town that could cut into what we do. It could be that we need 15 staff members for some program and we just lost two of them yesterday. In all those cases, the executive team identifies the problems and helps come up with solutions so everyone else can help the kids.

Because of all these responsibilities, communication within the business is very important. At the clinical level, all the frontline staff need to be in touch with coordinators, who need to be in touch with their VPs, and all the way back down.

Beyond that, communication within the company is also important for addressing new opportunities. At Children's Home, we sometimes have contracts with the Department of Corrections, for example. Maybe they're changing their programs around or they're offering some new funds to work together on a program. If that's the case, we're going to evaluate the program, see if it fits into our mission and flow, and then decide if we're going to put our name in the hat.

Or maybe we're going to meet with them to see if they'll tweak one of their programs so as not to duplicate one of ours, or maybe we'll combine it with one we already do, and so on.

Aside from internal meetings, the executive team is also required to serve on external committees—in their professional space and also statewide. These committees are sometimes coordinated with funders and organizations that could provide money for different services.

For example, our President and CFO is on a finance committee, which operates at the state level. In that committee, she can hear what members of the state government are thinking about and discussing for state budgets the following year. And she can also voice our concerns about how those changes would positively or negatively affect the kids in Peoria.

As CEO, I'm on 10 different local committees that are all tied to bettering our community. My focus is on PR, marketing and building relationships between Children's Home and different businesses—but every executive has their own specialties.

One committee that I'm on is about being an ambassador for Peoria. As part of our discussions in those meetings, I helped film a commercial talking about how great it is to live in Peoria, Illinois with the help of some other business experts in the room. In one sense, that doesn't have much at all to do with Children's Home. But in a broader sense, it does.

Lending my best efforts to advertising and participating in a commercial like that helps the community, which in turn helps us. Of course, not everybody has that philosophy. There are some CEOs and directors in those meetings who never do that kind of stuff—but some of us do it all. But I believe, ultimately, you have to believe in the bigger picture to do it.

Besides our own executive team, other people in these communities could include members of the local police, community leaders, business CEOs and other corporate figureheads who are community minded. Basically, it's all the community champions that need to know your story to help you run a successful nonprofit.

The guiding theory behind these committees is that you're only getting the best of the best when it comes to discussion, debate and expertise. Nobody in those rooms is there for resumé building—because nobody in those rooms needs to build a resumé. Still, one of the obstacles of having, say, 10 CEOs in a room means you might be dealing with 10 big egos.

In general, I find it helps to check your ego at the door and to know that they and we are there for the same reasons: to help kids in our community.

Though on the surface the executive team seems like "the bosses" of nonprofits, it's a little different than that. In my opinion, being a successful nonprofit executive is a lot like being a teacher or a firefighter in terms of the motivation behind it (or at least, it ought to be). You have to be there because you want to help.

Sometimes there are people who get into our business or serve on these committees because they have a personal connection to the mission. Other times, people get into it because they have the time and they want to help others. Above all though, this world needs more people who want to help. Life for at-risk groups is not getting easier in Peoria—or anywhere— and the problems need compassionate people to solve them.

In my experience, those with the greatest compassion are the most successful—and not just on the clinical level.

To be an effective nonprofit executive, you can't just be the stereotype of a ruthless or ego-driven businessman. You have to be compassionate at all times, and not just for the people you're serving. You need compassion for the people sitting next to you, and for the people sitting across the table.

I had a therapist tell me once that one of the hardest things about his career is that he needs a therapist of his own. I always found that interesting. The same is true for the people in our business. If you're working hands-on trying to solve the city's hardest problems, you're going to take it home with you.

And when you take it home with you, it's hard to relax at the end of the day and sit on the couch. You can't tell your kids everything about what you do either. If you're an executive, you have to carry all that responsibility with grace and a smile.

When people ask me what I do, I give my executive answer: "My job is to help people."

The Board

When we talk about a social service agency like Children's Home, it's simple to grasp what the clinical staff does. It's also easy to understand the responsibilities of the executive team. But no matter what, a nonprofit board is always the most invisible layer of a nonprofits — and one that deserves more attention.

In my experience, the board is one of the most underutilized pieces of a nonprofit. In many organizations, the instinct is to look at board meetings as a nuisance or something you have to do. "Oh, I'm dreading this board meeting," some executives might say.

I've never understood that at all.

I've never understood how a CEO can get to their position without understanding how to befriend and utilize the wisdom of a good board. But honestly, sometimes the problem is even simpler than that. What I've often seen on the most basic level is the failure to put together a big enough, broad enough board *at all*.

In some organizations, you might have a board that's just one or two members. But if you have a board with 20 members on it, you're talking about 20 professionals who know more than you in their area of expertise. As CEO, that's the philosophy that I bring to Children's Home when it comes to our board.

Whenever we need anything, we know we can call our board. But I guess we're getting a little ahead of ourselves.

If the staff is in the trenches and the executive team are the ones leading them into battle, the board members are like the generals or the spiritual advisors. They might not always work directly in the same line of work as your mission, but they've almost always built their own successful businesses in other areas. They're usually community leaders and people that others look up to.

When a board is assembled correctly, they're an invaluable resource.

At Children's Home, I'm involved with two boards—the trustee board (or the governing board) and the foundation board. Though both are important, they have some key differences.

Essentially, behind Children's Home is a foundation where money and financial gifts can go towards funding our programs. The foundation takes care of all the dollars raised for Children's Home through wills, estate gifts, special events and so on.

Per our bylaws, that foundation has its own board.

The trustees, meanwhile, are more involved with looking at the technical aspects of the business—

meaning the actual flow of finances in and out of programs, the audits, the risk factors and so on. If I were
to be disciplined or terminated, it would be a decision
voted on by the board of trustees. In a trustee meeting,
everyone sits down and maps out how to actually run
the business.

In the case of both boards, all members are volun-
teers. And at Children's Home, I'm the only employee
who reports to the trustee board.

Because we're a large organization that has pro-
duced results for 153 years in Illinois, I feel our board
is the best in town. Every single person at any of those
meetings is an expert at what they do, who brings
years of experience to the discussion. In both cases,
the board members are expected to attend and partic-
ipate in meetings at all phases of our business—from
development to finance and everything in between.

I've known plenty of CEOs who want to be 100
percent hands-off with the board or want the board to
be hands-off when it comes to the business. To me,
that's just stupid. To be as successful as possible, you
need to surround yourself at all times with people
who are smarter than you. And to that end, you need
a diverse board. You don't want to just have 15 bankers on your board, for example.

In our case, we have warriors. We have people in
manufacturing, project management and marketing.
We have doctors, strategic planners, real estate agents,
bankers and so many more. Right now, I think we

even have two or three attorneys. The point is that you want to assemble a wealth of different types of knowledge, and you want to go for the best business minds that you can get.

There's an old stereotype that business leaders make their money, retire and go sit on a board. "Let me go work at a pet shelter," someone might say. "Let me go work at the YMCA." There's a misconception that people join boards to avoid boredom, but that's not been my experience—and those certainly aren't people want on your board.

Board members have been very hands-on in most of the boards I've worked with. It comes down to the management, which means that if you're vetting potential business leaders to sit on your board, you better have a plan in mind for how to use their expertise.

If you recruit a great board member, but you don't have a role in mind for them, that's a big mistake. None of those members are getting paid, and together they have so much combined knowledge. It's free mentorship, advice and guidance for the company and the executive leadership (in other words, for me). And it comes in handy all the time.

I recently sat down with my board to try and get some advice about an upcoming fundraising event. There are political and strategic concerns at play when planning these events, and I came across a situation that stumped me. In the meeting, I had two different business leaders offer two radically different approaches. Each thought the problem over and gave me the best solution they had.

The beauty of that scenario was that after that meeting, I took the most important pieces from each one, and went on my way with a new solution.

Another time, I met with a board member who worked in real estate to talk about our facilities, our leases and the properties we owned. One of the most expensive parts about running a nonprofit can be the property costs and upkeep. I was interested in evaluating that at Children's Home, and was curious how cost-effective we were being.

He was able to show me where we could be more efficient, pointing out places where we were probably overpaying, and other places where we could combine and reorganize our facilities to be more streamlined. He had elegant solutions for problems that would've taken me forever to solve on my own. He gave me another point of view, and he gave my team options to consider.

I challenge CEOs and directors to put a dollar amount on expert advice like that. I would also say: Talk to a board member or a donor in some business capacity every day.

While most business decisions fall on the shoulders of the CEO, a smart CEO will get buy-in or backing from their finance committee or their board before making any big decisions—decisions like purchasing a building, a major personnel restructuring or making a major program change.

The board is a vital resource outside of a business context as well. They're people to make friends with and to learn from. I've had board members call me in really tough times just to talk, to check on me and see how I was doing. That kind of personal support is invaluable.

Putting together a good board and humbly seeking their advice is a huge responsibility for a good nonprofit CEO. A truly great board is that invisible ingredient that can help a good nonprofit organization turn into a great one.

Chapter 6:
501(c)(3) Facelift

Rebranding Nonprofits

As I've made abundantly clear by now, the public image of nonprofits comes with some baggage.

In one way, these organizations have people not taking them seriously as "real businesses." Then there are those who view them sympathetically and with pity, but don't want to engage. There's also the history of some nonprofits as tax havens or places where money gets spent inefficiently that can make younger and more politically minded talent view them skeptically.

Without a doubt, it's time for a serious rebranding of nonprofits so that people can appreciate what they do and how they work in the modern world. And one of the biggest potential solutions to all of these problems—and a big piece of the nonprofit sector rebrand is how we tell stories.

Storytelling is a facet of this business that touches everything we do. When you're talking about the image or the brand of an agency, you have to talk about the story they're telling.

It all starts with painting a positive picture.

Although some people say that if a thing is good enough it doesn't need marketing, they're only partially correct. That rule really only works with vices or things that people are impulsively inclined towards. Unfortunately, not all people are impulsively inclined towards social service. Even if they are, it's not natural for the media to gravitate towards happy and productive stories that tell people about it.

When I came onboard at Children's Home in 2014, it was a hidden gem in the community. Without a doubt, the organization was doing good work, had tons of supporters and great relationships with donors. But we weren't telling the story I thought we could tell.

We were doing good work but didn't have a consistent brand. I knew Children's Home shouldn't be a hidden gem. That was one of the first things I wanted to focus on fixing. I knew we were doing incredible things and we could do even more if the community clearly understood our mission.

One of our biggest supporters and champions reached out to a branding company that their business had used. This company has worked with some of the largest Fortune 500 companies in the world. The branding company agreed to help us. They came in and worked with our team at Children's Home for what ended up being a three-year period.

Obviously social service-oriented nonprofits don't tend to have a lot of extra money in the budget for marketing and image overhauls. Fortunately, this group agreed to come in and start the rebranding recommendation process. It worked out for everyone involved, but it all started from the strength of Children's Home's local business relationships.

It was one of the most important first things we did when I came onboard.

When the branding company came in, the first thing they did was research. They started the process by sending out questionnaires about us to community leaders in Peoria. They wanted to know the general impression of Children's Home. When you invite that type of feedback and welcome the perspectives of your donors, you end up finding out some pretty blunt things about what you're doing wrong.

Though there were plenty of positive responses about our programs and services, there were some negatives as well. There was confusion about our overall message and exactly what we do. There was also a lack of clarity on some points about just how well we do certain things. We were doing things really well, but a lot of people just didn't know.

Essentially it was market research—we were getting a better picture about our place in the community, and areas to improve our brand. It was no different than what a for-profit would do.

What we gathered was that we had a great reputation and people seemed to know we were an excellent agency. However, the community was not as clear as we thought about what we actually do and the services we offer. That became one focus area in our rebranding.

We then brought in some of the key stakeholders and different leaders throughout the agency to gather their opinions. The branding team met with our executive team repeatedly over the course of two years to figure out how to change our approach and storytelling.

We were talking about strategy and branding most of all. We talked about where Children's Home fit in the community, who our competitors were and so on. They helped us to identify keywords and phrases that cut through the noise and got to the heart of our story. Though I would never want to give away all the ingredients to the secret sauce, some of those keywords are phrases I still use all the time.

Out of that process emerged the messages I have already shared. That Children's Home is a large, multi-faceted, best-in-class agency.

Rebranding Children's Home was one of the most exhilarating processes of my life. Getting an insight into how Fortune 500 companies presented themselves and applying those lessons to what we do was beyond eye opening. I learned more from working with them through that process than I did in a lot of my college classes.

On the strength of Children's Home's mission and leveraging our relationships with the local business community, we gained access to a lot of benefits. When you consider what companies typically spend for their rebrands coming in cold, the value of that experience was astronomical.

Out of respect to our partner who facilitated this relationship and gave us this opportunity, all I can say is thank you and we appreciate you more than you'll ever know.

Attitude Adjustments

There's obviously an element of outside perspective that comes into play when running a big nonprofit, but there's internal work that needs to be done as well. One of the big misconceptions about nonprofit agencies is that they rely on handouts, hand-me-downs and have to scrape and scrimp to accomplish their aims.

Though it's important to change the outside world's perspective about those tropes, it's also important to shift that perspective internally with your team. And to change it for those you hope to hire. After all, if the perception of the business is that it's tough and low paying, you have to be able to justify yourself to the talent you wish to attract.

The job can be emotionally draining, and understandably so. As such, the passion and compassion piece is huge for me. In the business of helping people, you have to put yourself in the shoes of your employees more often than you do in a for-profit.

In the case of Children's Home, what we have to do is to constantly and continually refresh and retell our story—and that's been the case for the entire 153 years we've been operational.

Some CEOs ask, "How do other people look at our business?" But I say, "Let's tell them what we do at Children's Home on a daily basis. Let's brag about what we do well, but let's also tell them about the issues." It comes from a more personal and honest place, and the focus isn't on external opinion.

After all, we're going to do the work regardless of what people think about it.

There are plenty of issues in the social service sector, and newspapers and websites like to talk about all the bad things because they tend to sell better. You're likely to hear a lot of stories about violence and the people the system failed. But if you dig deeper, how these kids and families got into the system in the first place is its own story.

A lot of the time, that element of the story gets lost at a typical fundraiser or marketing event. The story is a lot more focused on the things that can draw immediate sympathy, things that are the most shocking or the most easily understandable.

For the social service sector, that often translates to using struggling or suffering babies and young children to sell a mission.

You see it all the time. It's a video, an appeal or a PSA. Any kind of message that comes at the world directly, trying to sell something. But they always use a hungry baby or a crying little kid. Though that's definitely a real part of the problems we deal with, it's not all of it.

The bottom line is we have a lot of kids and families who flow through our agency every month. And when they do, the average kid is 14 years old. Right away, that's not as easy a story to tell—but it's more accurate.

And in some ways, it's a more important part of the story that isn't getting addressed.

When I'm at fundraisers or I'm out in the community, I like to tell stories about kids who are 16, 17 and 18. I tell stories about kids who have been dealing with hardships for a long time, kids who have been in the system for their whole lives and who have survived despite all the odds. I tell those stories because these kids don't stay kids forever. I say this a lot, but those kids grow up. Eventually, they become adults.

And once you're an adult, you reach a crossroads of whether you're going to go the right way or the wrong way.

I get why different agencies market themselves with shock tactics. It's an in-your-face way of raising money, and sometimes that's what people want to see—the kids who are malnourished or families that need a home. While I understand that piece, the reality is that it's a very small part of the big picture. And it's really the part of the nonprofit sector that could use some rebranding across the board.

There's a big image gap, and it produces a kind of empathy gap as well.

It's easy to feel sympathy for babies and little kids, but it's a little harder to take responsibility for a teenager who has been through hard life experiences and made some mistakes as a result. It's hard to champion those people that the system has left behind. But it's our job to try.

Similarly, there's also an image gap when it comes to bringing people onboard. It's not a gap you can fill by telling people they're going to be cowboys or anything like that, but you can fill it from a "changing lives and saving lives" perspective.

If there's a young adult who has his heart set on working for the CIA, there's probably not an easy way to convince him to change course. On the other hand, there are plenty of people out there who have the right skills for social work that could be convinced to pursue it with the right marketing and storytelling. And the first time those people have a hand in saving a life or a family, they will get a feeling most people never get to feel.

I can attest that it's a feeling that can change your entire life.

On a team like ours, we have people who have been with us for 30 to 40 years, and I think that speaks to the quality of our culture. Still, I don't see many people coming into the business now that will be around in 40 years. These days, I hope for five—and it's a major blessing if we get them for 10.

That has to change.

I don't know if or when it will, but when it comes to the idea of rebranding, these are all the important pieces the nonprofit sector needs to consider.

Big Asks and Business Partnerships

When we're thinking about these big branding issues in a nonprofit, we have to look at which methods and strategies to use to change them. Though no one person has all the answers, there are a lot of ways to go about changing our stories and changing our image.

A lot of the methods we've had success with at Children's Home have to do with close relationships with the business community and making big asks.

I always joke that I'm told "no" way more often than I'm told "yes," but I never get upset about it because nobody makes as many asks as I do.

No one person can save all the kids that need saving—it takes a team. And beyond our team, it takes the support of the wider community. That includes the business community. To that end, it pays to be grateful and appreciative to your donors, your community leaders and your business leaders. Many of them are just as concerned about the community as you are, and relationships with them are important to everyone's wellbeing.

Nonprofits make mistakes by not forging those kinds of relationships early enough and when running their organization like a single program rather than a full company. If you don't sit down and figure out specifically where you want to go to and how to get there, it's going to be a much steeper hill to climb in the long run.

There are plenty of times in business and in nonprofit work where you can add a ton of value to your organization through your relationships. Still, there also comes a point where you have to make a big ask to accomplish what you want. But to be in that position, you must first have great mutual respect with the people you approach. You have to be tied together in the community.

And secondly, you must know what you need— and have a specific ask in mind.

If you get a meeting with a Fortune 500 CEO, you really need to have a plan and a specific ask ready for that meeting before you sit down at the table. You can't just walk in for idle conversation and you can't give a generalized pitch describing what you do. You need a strategy going in, and you need an ongoing communication plan for everybody within the company.

To expand on that, you also need great internal systems for keeping track of all your donors and supporters. Though the reason should be obvious, it doesn't hurt to state it explicitly:

Your donors and supporters are hugely responsible for why you accomplish your mission, and they deserve your gratitude and respect.

But it goes beyond that. Your donors aren't just people who wrote you a check, they're essentially your partners in a cause. They're your friends and neighbors, and they're all individuals with their own attachments to your mission. You have to treat them that way to keep your relationships healthy and strong.

And to do that, you need to be organized.

You need to have a database and a system for collating your donors and supporters that you can reference and scroll through with ease. At Children's Home, we have systems in place that allow me pull up the top 20 donors of the past five, 10, 15 and 20 years with the click of a button.

Even with that level of access and organization, sometimes the top 20 donors aren't the ones you need to talk to in a given situation. Maybe it's someone else who isn't as closely tied to you yet. You need to know how to analyze donor data, examine the ones you have the clearest paths to and then make the right asks.

Aside from your outside donors and supporters, this is another area where utilization of key board members can come in really handy. A good board has much collective expertise, but it also has many community connections that can be tapped.

As a leader and a CEO, you start this process by identifying areas where you can offer your leadership capabilities. You need to know and capitalize on your own strengths, but you also have to identify your weaknesses. With that in mind, you have to start mapping those weaknesses onto your networks and business connections.

Within those networks, you need to find people who are strong where you're weak. Seek out mutually beneficial relationships.

A good leader will know that they can't accomplish their mission alone. They also know that you never have the budget to accomplish your mission. That goes for most entrepreneurs and nonprofit leaders in general. In general, a good leader is willing to think big—bigger than their pockets allow. But when you're thinking that way, the next step is to start thinking socially and creatively—and that's where most people drop the ball.

Agencies can get stagnant if they're not being prosocial, if they're not forging relationships and they're not making big strategic asks. Once you start talking to your board, taking your donors out to dinner and shaking hands in the community, you can get a lot of information. You can start picking a lot of people's brains and building relationships, and there's no telling what can come from that. Sometimes it's better communication, or maybe it's more donors, it could even be a pro bono contract. But there's no limit to what can come from that kind of positive approach.

Another great example of this is how Children's Home was able to work with Caterpillar.

From the outside, people may know Caterpillar for their great work building top-of-the-line construction equipment and machines and selling them all over the world. Though that's definitely true, what people might not know is how top-of-the-line Caterpillar is when it comes to organization and project management. They're second to none, and it was an area we were struggling with at Children's Home when I came onboard.

So, I went to Caterpillar with a big ask.

It wasn't that we were asking for money; we were asking for their expertise. We wanted to get in touch with their director of project management, and we managed to get a meeting with him. I told him that although Children's Home had a lot of great ideas, we weren't always the best at mobilizing and executing them.

Sometimes we would come up with a good idea and then procrastinate. After that, there would be a bunch of meetings that would come and go and we'd find ourselves asking, "Whatever happened with that project?" We didn't have enough formalized internal processes. We needed a system to take our widely diverse project ideas and make them more executable and deliverable.

We asked the Caterpillar team to help us become more efficient and gain a better understanding of project management.

In business, you'll sometimes hear about business leaders and executive teams going through Six Sigma training for process improvement in manufacturing, for example. But project management is an entirely different animal. After thinking it over, the team at Caterpillar found a way to make it mutually beneficial and they offered their help.

Over the course of three years, we worked with Caterpillar to learn their processes and we gradually implemented the Caterpillar project management model at Children's Home. Still, we tweaked it to cater to our business. That partnership took our business to an entirely new level.

There are multiple important lessons in that story.

The first thing is that Children's Home and Caterpillar had always had a mutual relationship and a respect. The second is that we didn't go to the meeting with them and ask: "Can you donate $10 million?" That would've been a short-term solution to a problem, and something that wasn't scalable (or very attractive to Caterpillar, either).

Instead, we asked their team of project managers to donate some of their time over a multi-year period to teach and develop our team. That kind of ask is worth more in the long run than any cash figure anyway.

It's hard to go to someone and make a specific ask for your cause, but it's even harder to identify and face where your business is particularly weak. We had to look at where we were weakest, identify it and ask how we could get better. We talked to our board and our supporters, and then we went out into the community.

Now, we have a dedicated person for project management at Children's Home and the whole ship runs more smoothly.

Out of that experience, we've implemented systems that have given our entire leadership team a boost. One example is having a "cadence" as we call it, a once-a-week meeting with the whole leadership team to review projects, and that will never change as long as I'm CEO. It's vital in getting everyone on the same page and it only takes 30 minutes. We do a quick review of what's in the works and what's happening in the project management process. It has completely changed our business.

But the other thing worth mentioning is those asks and those relationships can have unintended bonus effects for your business as well.

The bonus is that at Children's Home, making big asks *within* the organization has become a part of our culture as well. In some stagnant organizations, the culture is limiting when it comes to free expression and suggesting new ideas. We wanted to change that. We didn't want our team to think: "Here we go again, another big project that won't get implemented." We knew we needed to add some incentives to get people to buy-in.

We made the decision that we would open our project management program up to anybody who wanted to complete it at any position within our company. Anybody had the opportunity to pitch an idea for a new project could fill out a request and submit it to the leadership team. Through that, we ended up training more than 70 employees in Project Management 101. The best part about it is that our own employees from all levels got the chance to work with Caterpillar's best project managers one-on-one (thanks to their generosity).

After all these changes, the bottom line is we're never going to take on a project without knowing we can do it as efficiently as possible. In the first year that Caterpillar did this with us, we were even recognized for our efforts.

There's a worldwide group called Project Management Institute (PMI), and they give out awards every year for the best model partnerships between social service agencies and Fortune 500 companies.

The idea behind these awards is to encourage and honor the work done between the for-profit and non-profit sectors in improving project management processes across the world.

That first year, I flew out to San Diego with Caterpillar's team and we beat out all kinds of other Fortune 500 companies. Working together, Caterpillar and Children's Home won an award for implementing the Caterpillar model to run our organization more efficiently. It was one of the biggest honors I've ever been a part of, and it was a huge boost to the entire team.

But the point of all this is not to brag. It's to show how vital these relationships and big asks really are. Above all, it's not just about getting money from people. It's about building relationships and adding value.

Chapter 7:
A New Mission

Make the Mission Come Alive

It gets pretty hard to talk about social service and non-profits without talking a lot about *mission*. When these organizations were invented, civic-minded groups were pooling their efforts behind common ideals, ones that would make the world around them a better place. When social service was mostly happening on a tight-knit, community level, it was pretty hard to veer away from your mission.

After all, if you're a small group of people volunteering with the local church to give food to the needy in your neighborhood, there's not much ambiguity there.

You're either doing what you're supposed to be doing, or you're not.

But as the nonprofit sector has grown and grown, there's been more and more confusion about the mission. It's easy enough to see what an organization says their mission is, but sometimes it harder to see how well they're executing it. It can also be unclear if the people working at the organization truly feel like they're in line with the mission. This especially becomes a problem when an organization is trying to get new people to join.

It's hard to get people to back your mission if you don't have a clear vision for yourself.

That's why I always say you have to make the mission come alive—it's a very important piece of the nonprofit puzzle.

Some of the oldest charities and social service organizations actually have the word "mission" in their name. The word even carries militaristic and spiritual connotations. If I say that someone is a missionary, people have a pretty clear picture of how that looks. Chances are you're picturing some kind of monk-like figure, dedicated to their principles and living in solitude or traveling the world to spread their message.

Now, that's not quite the spirit of what we do and who we are—but that model of intensity and dedication is a good reminder of what the word means. At Children's Home, our official mission is to give kids a childhood and a future by protecting them. Our mission is to teach and heal them, and to build strong communities and strong families.

When we hire employees, I flat out tell people in orientation exactly what we're about at Children's Home. I let them know that the kids are their number one priority, but that they also need to be there for each other. Although there are plenty of well-intentioned people who want to get involved, if our employees don't have those two ingredients, they're just not going to make it in our business.

The bottom line is that everyone who works at Children's Home has a passion for helping. Of course, finding a lot of those kinds of people can be difficult. But it's so important.

If you can find those people, they become the lifeblood of the organization.

When it comes to developing a frontline staff, it's hard to find people who are going to last for the long haul because it's such a hard job. So, when we do interviews, we have to present a very clear understanding of our mission, and we have to show how good our outcomes are. When we do our interviews, we look for people who have a variety of different backgrounds and a wide array of experiences.

But ultimately, it all boils down to passion and compassion—and they have to have both.

Mission is Passion at Work

Even after finding the right people to work at your organization, the mission isn't something that happens in an abstract way or something that happens over time. Mission happens day in, day out, every day at your organization (if you're doing it right). At least, that's the ideal we strive for.

A saying I have when it comes to the mission is that mission is passion at work.

While sometimes that work is easy for the community to the see, a lot of the time it isn't. That's because the work that nonprofits do is making the mission happen at all levels, all the time. Even the mundane tasks that people don't want to do.

And even the things that happen behind the scenes.

Our frontline staff interviews are very thorough when it comes to screening for skills, passion and compassion, and that level of screening runs all the way through our organization. Our interviews for the maintenance and kitchen teams are just as thorough, and we're looking for all the same things.

We recently hired someone for our kitchen team. In the middle of the interview, the person said, "I know I can probably make more money somewhere else because I'm a cook, but I saw this as an opportunity to give back because I always wanted to help somebody. I took this as a chance to change gears in my life."

That's a quality that's very hard to bullshit, if you'll pardon my French.

Those are the kinds of people who will go above and beyond for the mission. In the case of Children's Home, it means people who are going to be there for the executive team, for each other and for the kids. You'll always find people like that in this line of work if you look hard enough, but you need to be thorough and dedicated to finding them.

Caseworkers or therapists may be able to make a bigger salary somewhere else, like a hospital. But the bottom line is that they come to organizations like ours because they're interested in choosing mission over job. They're taking fulfillment over the money. Those are the kinds of people you want by your side, and those are the kinds of people you need to honor above all others.

When I talk to new hires, I always say I want them to think of what they're doing as the beginning of a career or a calling, not just a job.

A job is something you do just to make some money and to make ends meet—and there are plenty of opportunities like that out there in the world. A career is something you dedicate yourself to, something you build over a lifetime. And a calling is something even more special and elusive. It's something you do because you know it's the right thing for you, deep down. It's something you can't help but do, no matter how hard it is.

For many people, their tenure at Children's Home ends up only being a job or a short-lived position from which they eventually transition. That's just the nature of the beast. But for the people who do give it their all, there's nothing more rewarding.

I had someone in my office recently asking if there was any way they could get a raise. We were talking about what this person brought to the organization, how dedicated they had been and how the extra money would make a big difference in their life. After all of our talking, it turned out that this person had been working at Children's Home for 25 years—a quarter of a century!

It was clear from our conversation that to this person, it wasn't just a job. It was a career.

There are plenty of people who get their master's degree after spending five or six long years in school and they come out ready to start their life. They're looking for a job or a career that's going to give them stability, maybe something that will allow them to start a family. In the current market, unemployment is low and job growth seems as good as ever.

If you have a master's degree, you're in a position where you can pretty much write your own ticket. Though that higher degree is bound to make these people valuable assets anywhere, they come to Children's Home because of the reputation we've built and the mission we've outlined.

It's therefore our job to make that mission as clear as possible, to create a company culture where we nurture that mission. When that's all done, we need to honor the work and the sacrifices these people are putting in all the time.

With all that in place, the final piece is to know what to look for when you're recruiting—and to know exactly how to sell the mission.

Selling the Mission

When you're recruiting, you obviously have to tell people what the work entails—but you have to tell them in a specific way. You have to sell them on the mission, but also paint an enticing picture. You're not selling them a job; you're selling them a life. You have to say: "You're not going to get stuck in one place, you're going to grow. Here's the vision."

When it comes to the mission, this is the hardest part.

If you were to get a job at Caterpillar, you could start in janitorial services, do a great job, get recognized and work your way all the way up in the company. In organizations like that, there's a clear ladder and a step-by-step process you can follow if you're ambitious to achieve more and move up.

In a nonprofit organization, it's not always like that.

If you're a caseworker, in most situations, you're going to keep being a caseworker. Because of the way that field is structured, there's not always a clear growth path. That's not to say that you can't start as a caseworker at an organization like Children's Home and move your way up, but it's a concern you need to address during the interview process. Ultimately, no matter your position in our organization, you'll have an opportunity to grow.

On the other hand, it's important to show the frontline staff that they're not going to be stagnant in their jobs, either—they're still going to grow. If you were to pick a for-profit job in another area, say at Walmart for example, you would know what you'd be doing day in, day out for a long time. There would be a ton of stability and predictability there and it wouldn't change much on a day-to-day basis.

At a nonprofit, that's just not true at all—which can be an exciting selling point for the right person.

If you were to shadow someone at Children's Home, what they were doing at that moment would be totally different five minutes later, and a half hour from then, and so on. The next day would also look totally new compared to the one before. Crises arise all the time and the people we work with need to be nimble, able to problem solve and put out fires—there's intrigue in that.

It doesn't matter who you are or what position you're in. At Children's Home, there's always a new issue to face. Our employees aren't going to be living their lives like it's *Groundhog Day*—facing the same issues every single day. Everything is individualized and always changing.

You can hook talent with that, and you can hook them on the passion and compassion piece.

If you're interviewing people that are just coming out of school and are in the process of getting their Master's, you may need to remind them that there is a path for growth and a life for them in the nonprofit world (if that's something they're looking for). In other situations, you may have to level with them that the casework is going to be the majority of what they're signing up for—how it's presented depends on the person

The bottom line is that a lot of people come out of school with a lot of debt. They have to figure out how to do the mission, do their job and still live their lives. To that end, it makes sense why it's tough to recruit good people. In nonprofits, the majority of the money is going to programs, and *after* that it's going to people who work within programs.

In a similar for-profit organization, insurance money and profit incentives mean that a therapist or a clinician can make a lot more money working in a particular niche. Nonprofits have a hard time competing with those benefits, but for-profits have their own problems as well.

Taking a silo approach to healthcare and behavioral health can mean more specialization and money for the people working in those areas. But it can also mean higher costs for the people who need services, and a breakdown of outcomes on a systemic level.

I don't think either model works perfectly as is, and there are always ways to improve. There's a reason why nonprofits are the way they are, and they do care about taking care of their frontline staff as much as possible. It's just a hard problem to solve. And the other fact of the matter is simple: Nonprofit work just isn't for everybody.

We had a hiring fair recently where about 40 people came by to see what we were about. I think we hired five out of the 40. That's not a bad success rate at the end of the day. On the other hand, there are 35 people who said "no" to what we had to offer, or who just weren't the right fit.

That's part of the game, and it's something to be prepared for.

When you're in a smaller town like Peoria instead of a metropolis like Chicago, New York or LA, the pool is smaller. And the pool starts to get cannibalized, in a sense. There might be so many nonprofits in a small area that the employees are getting recycled between organizations. In that market, there's a big need for people and a lot of opportunities for them to jump ship.

Sometimes employees think the grass is greener on the other side. On the other hand, you'll also get people who leave to go test themselves and end up coming back. There are many different situations, but the fact is that finding and retaining good people is hard work.

Selling the mission is key to doing both parts successfully.

You have to be aware of the market you're in. If you're in a rural town, sometimes it's not the people that are hard to come by—it's the funding and the donors. In a big city, you have a bigger funding pool but a ton of competing organizations and duplicated services. It's a mixed bag either way.

The situation with nonprofits is a little like the situation with nursing right now. There aren't a lot of people getting into the field, and it's a bit of an epidemic. As a sector, nonprofits are going to have to change to find and recruit more people. And once we get them, we're going to have to come up with creative ways to retain them.

There was a time around 10 years ago where the labor market was a little different. You typically didn't have a lot of job openings and there wasn't as much mobility and movement for employees. I think right now, finding quality employees is becoming a more serious issue—sometimes even on a month-to-month basis—and this isn't a Children's Home problem, it's a problem nationwide.

One of the biggest worries a nonprofit organization tends to have is that they'll have a good candidate come in, complete their training and move on to something they think is bigger and better. That's a huge stress on the system and it comes at the cost to the people you're serving—in our case, the kids. We already have stress points when it comes to training, so to add that on top makes things even harder. We like to think we help people on their career paths, and we definitely want people thinking big. But we also want them to stay around.

There's a level of frustration when we lose somebody after just a year and a half, or you've spent several years training and honing somebody's skills only to have them leave. There's so much mentorship that goes into employees that ultimately benefits another organization. It's a big hit to team morale. We end up questioning ourselves. What did we do wrong? What could we have done better?

It's hard to say what the answer is, and maybe some of it is just the nature of the beast. But we can't just throw our hands in the air.

To combat that loss and that brain drain, we have to add in benefits, incentives and flexibility however we can at all levels to keep people engaged. We have to create a good culture and we need a brand that employees want to be part of, one they can wear proudly.

We need to assure people that they'll experience radical growth and that they won't stagnate, even if their title stays the same. Sometimes, we also need to show people that there's a path to move through the organization.

There are plenty of strategies to use and things to consider. But the bottom line is that it all flows from the mission, a mission that it's our job to sell.

Chapter 8:
Recruiting and Sales

Recruiting the Best

Once an organization is clear about its priorities and its mission, it's time to build the team to execute that mission. Knowing where to start can be a daunting task. In addition to the difficulties of finding and keeping good people, there's also the challenge of knowing how to organize them once they're in place.

What's important to know is that recruiting and sales go hand-in-hand. And also that once you've got your mission clear, a lot of what you need to fill out becomes self-evident.

All the directors at a company are going to have their agency's core positions dictated by the programs they run. For example, if you're running a lot of behavioral health programs, you need a lot of caseworkers and therapists. The situation with foster care is pretty similar—you're going to need house managers, caseworkers and people who know how to take care of kids. All of that is pretty self-explanatory.

Upper management is really dictated by the CEO. The organization's leader is going to build out a team around them who complements their talents and strengths—and not just people who are going to be yes-men.

You want to hire people whose strengths are your weaknesses.

I'm a true believer in letting yourself feel like the dumb guy in a room. In other words, it's best to keep yourself surrounded by people who are smarter than you at whatever it is they do—and never let that be a threat to your ego. If you're an effective leader, you recognize that teamwork is the best way to fulfill the mission. It's not about showboating or being a cowboy.

Though it's a given that you want executive leaders who complement one another, you also want to be careful with egos. In nonprofit work especially, everybody needs to learn to leave their egos at the door when they sit together to solve problems. While it's understandable that leaders at that level could have a big ego (and they often need to use those egos to get things done), they have to at least be willing to collaborate and listen when necessary.

I do believe all the members of Children's Home are equally important at the deepest level. Still, there were still a few key positions in leadership I knew I needed to pay close attention to when I was in the reorganization stages. They were roles that needed to complement my leadership style.

From my standpoint, two of the most important shifts were making the CFO the *President* and CFO, and to make our former IT Director a VP of IT and Facilities.

When I came onboard at Children's Home, it was technically as *President* and CEO. However, we already had somebody in the CFO position that had a vast wealth of knowledge, somebody who had already been doing great work at the organization. I felt that she should be promoted, and the position I felt was right was my title of President. I had board members question my decision-making, but I never once questioned myself.

From my view, the CFO is a position that can make or break an agency. Though the CEO is the public face and the person who's often publicly scrutinized, in many ways the CFO has a more complex and technical job to do. A good CFO does more than anyone can imagine because their job is so complex.

A normal accountant would focus on a certain area of the business or a certain aspect of auditing. A good CFO, in the case of Children's Home, focuses on everything from timetables to receivables, auditing, grants and contracts. There's also the company's cash flow, banking, insurance and payroll to worry about. Beyond that, they also need to have a great relationship with the board and the company's HR department.

It's way more than a numbers position—though it is that, too.

When you look at it a certain way, the entire business is really run through the CFO in concert with the HR department—they're in charge of recruiting, retention and payroll. The CFO has to have a clear picture of the financial health of the agency at all times, and they have to clearly communicate that picture to the rest of the executive team as well.

Beyond technical skills, you need somebody who's both knowledgeable about the field and ethical. You want someone who has a core set of principles from which they won't waver. In essence, you're hiring a CFO almost as if they were a second CEO. That person becomes the CEO's other half, and they have to work closely together. And at Children's Home, we have a great one in our President and CFO, Melissa Riddle.

The VP of IT and Facilities was another important shift. Once again, that was a person who had been at the organization for more than 20 years. He also had a great business mind, so it gave me a new perspective from a technology standpoint (which is not my strongest area).

Though it's an easy thing for inexperienced organizations to overlook, IT is so important for many reasons.

In today's day and age, the larger your agency is, the more phones and computers and servers and so on that you'll need. Aside from making sure the communication lines within your agency are working perfectly, there's also a lot of highly sensitive information flowing through the company's servers and computers at all times. Anytime you have that kind of information flowing around, it makes you a target for hackers, ransomware, viruses and whatever other kinds of technological threats may be out there.

For those reasons and more, a great IT director is invaluable. A good director in that position can build a great architecture to keep all parts of your company running smoothly—and they can protect you against digital threats that could compromise your donors, your customers and your business in general. What also makes it a little different from other executive leadership positions is that whoever is in there needs to be on the spot at all times. After all, a cyber security crisis can pop up without any warning.

Having the right software and keeping it updated is not optional for a big agency—it's essential. For that reason, there's a close relationship and synergy between your IT director and your CFO as well. After all, the accounting department and HR use complex programs which house a lot of data, and they all need to be working as well as possible to be successful.

You need someone who can juggle many different internal systems at once, who knows how to make all those different systems speak to one another. Beyond that, you also need a person who can handle all the many state and federal contracts your agency is juggling from a technological perspective. The records need to be kept orderly and secure, or many aspects of the business can be compromised. It's definitely a hard hire. You need a jack-of-all-trades.

Though I knew those two would be important positions, in reality all of the leadership positions have extremely complex and crucial responsibilities in the organization. Another major one at Children's Home is the Clinical Director, who in our agency is the Executive VP. After all, that person needs to have a comprehensive clinical background and strong knowledge about programs. They need to make sure all the different programs available at the agency are working in concert with one another, and that each child's treatment teams are working to their benefit.

Their job is to make sure the clinical staff is behind the mission and on the same page with their clinical philosophy at all levels. Because that *is* Children's Home's "product," there's no underselling its importance.

Though I could go on and on, the idea is the same for all the rest of the leadership positions as well—each person needs to be able to do their job, to run a huge team and to make their department speak to all the other departments fluently.

Still, one part of the organization that has unique importance when it comes to development is the Human Resources department.

Developing a Team

Depending on the organization, the HR department can have a big or a relatively small role. In an innovative and cutting-edge agency, HR will at least have a seat at the table. But the more you can use that department, the better the business will be.

While a big part of building a nonprofit agency is developing your programs and services, another big part is developing your team and your staff—that means market research, competing for a limited talent pool and keeping people happy.

And that's where HR comes in.

The HR department needs to have a good grasp on your agency's staffing needs. Because people are coming and going from the nonprofit sector all the time, they need to keep your agency's temperature and communicate with the rest of the executive team about positions that might need to get filled soon. But from a more business-oriented perspective, they also need to stay up to date on what's going on in the market outside of your agency.

Even if a company thinks it knows what's going on in the market, plenty of positions are hard to fill under optimal conditions. Even in the best circumstances, it's hard to stay on top of salary scales and pay grades in a way that's economical for a company and competitive to the outside world. In the nonprofit sector, where compensation and advancement can already be a tough sell, that piece becomes especially important.

There's a lot of competition out there, and it's not only with other social service agencies. Nonprofits compete with schools, universities, hospitals and health departments for quality talent. All of those are businesses that do good in the community, but in another sense, they're all competitors when it comes to getting the best people.

And even if you get the best people, there's always a chance you might lose some of them to one of those competitors. The HR department needs to help the company stay on its toes on the labor front at all times.

Though HR will deal with the hiring, recruiting and the interpersonal issues among staff members, they also serve as a kind of glue between a lot of different parts of the organization. As mentioned, they have close ties to the CFO and to the finances of the organization in general—manpower is a huge cost, after all. On an individual level, they're integral to the team members' relationships with each other as well. As I've said again and again, the culture at a large nonprofit is a key component to its success. HR is also connected to the marketing and branding side of things as well.

While there is the problem of attracting top-tier talent to a sector that's a difficult sell on many fronts, the fact remains that nonprofits are growing faster than the for-profit sector. A big part of that has to do with a shift in economic conditions and social consciousness.

But it also has to do with the legacy and branding of certain nonprofits in particular.

At Children's Home, we've worked hard to develop a brand and an image that speaks to the community and to the depths of what we do. We're a large agency, we're best in class when it comes to outcomes and we're engaged in the community. In a sector where there's rapid turnover, we have people that have stayed working with us for 20 to 40 years at a time—in all kinds of different positions.

When it comes to building and developing an organization, that message and that brand needs to be communicated clearly to do that. And HR plays an important role in regulating and protecting that message while the ball is rolling.

Children's Home has a story we tell about who we are, and it's one we've honed over 153 years of existence. And we sell it to our staff and to our community. Still, the truth is that we are far more than just one story. Where the sales element really comes into play is in choosing which story to tell which people at which time.

It's not just about telling a story—it's about telling the *right* story.

Telling the Right Story

As I've said again and again, being able to paint a clear picture of the vision of your organization is critical. And it's important early in the recruiting and onboarding process to start painting that vision.

I do a lot of storytelling in my job, both good and bad. Because that's the reality of what we're doing. In the early stages, I'll tell some feel-good stories because things can start out really tough, and happy endings definitely do happen. For people who are just getting their feet wet in this kind of work, those kinds of stories talk about big wins and making big differences, and they can really lift people's spirits.

But the stories that are tougher to hear can have the same impact and be just as motivating, depending on the situation. If the feel-good story's takeaway is, *we're doing so much good for these kids*; the tough story has a different takeaway.

That one says: That terrible thing might've happened to that kid, but it won't happen to any kid on my watch.

It's hard for me personally to get everyone telling their own stories and their own experiences. It's a little like the *E Pluribus Unum* idea that America is founded on—all the stories can be different, but when you weave them all together, you get one shining ideal that emerges. The stories people tell can all have different endings, but the themes are usually the same. No matter what business you're in, telling your story is a way to connect others to the spirit of the work and the mission.

And it's that type of storytelling that drives sales—selling your organization to your potential employees and selling it to your donors. Here's a story that I've told in both those contexts.

My hobby is cooking, always has been and always will be. It's one of my big stress relievers. One of my favorite things to cook is barbecue and I make all different kinds—but I especially like making pulled pork.

When I was little, my mom would make pulled pork barbecue along with these double chocolate chip sheet cookies in a pan. We'd serve it with cornbread on the side and it was one of my most cherished meals and memories from my childhood. I was always so grateful and felt lucky whenever my mom would take the time to make it.

One day, I ended up telling the Children's Home kids about those times cooking with my mom when I was little and how much I loved it. One of the kids asked me if I would make that same dinner for them sometime. Once the idea was presented to me, it seemed so obvious that I wondered why I hadn't thought of doing it before—of course I would make the kids dinner!

After that, I made barbecue for two different parts of our agency, and I did it exactly how my mom used to do it when I was little. I did it as a holiday surprise and everybody loved it. I felt good sharing that part of my story with the kids and for serving them in that way.

A couple months later, I was walking around and one of the kids came up to me. "Mr. George, Mr. George," he said. "Are you going to cook for us like that again? We've never had any of that barbecue stuff you made before and it was so good."

The kid saying this to me was 14 years old and I couldn't believe my ears. That a 14-year-old kid had never had homemade barbecue before put the entire act in perspective for me, and made me appreciate my own childhood even more. And the entire situation happened from the strength of an offhand story I told.

The whole thing made me think about how many things we all take for granted.

It's not the most heartwarming story I have, but hearing that kid talk about my barbecue like that knocked me in my gut and made me really think about some things.

But there are stories far sadder and more hopeful to tell, too.

As another example, we had another kid who basically grew up at Youth Farm, our residential facility. Kids who end up at Youth Farm are there because the state has parental rights. Their parents or family somehow gave up their rights and turned them over to the system. They used to be called "wards of the state," though they changed the name recently, thank God, to "youth in care."

At any rate, this young man was in care for years and had some anger issues. And what typically happens through that program is that the kids "age out" when they're 21 years old. Although we do everything we can for kids up until they become legal adults, it's hard to stay in contact with the people who leave our programs unless they want to be in contact with us. It's hard to follow them; in fact, it's nearly impossible.

Needless to say, he finished the program and fell off the map.

I was walking through downtown Peoria one winter a few years later, probably in about 2009. I was minding my own business when I looked down an alley and saw a homeless man sitting by himself. He had his hands up, a blanket over his head and we made eye contact—and I realized I recognized him.

He was the same kid who had been in Youth Farm his entire life.

He looked up and called me Mr. George, just like he used to. He was shocked and embarrassed that I was seeing him like that. He was hurt, and I was hurt as well. The moment was so surreal that it stopped me in my tracks. It felt like providence.

I'd been on my way to a lunch meeting, but I cancelled it. I helped the young man get a hotel room and told him to go upstairs and get cleaned up. After that,

I took him to get him some fresh clothes and something to eat. He was so grateful but the whole time I was questioning myself.

Where had we gone wrong?

After we had his basic needs taken care of, he told me his story. After leaving Youth Farm, he'd gotten a job and was doing okay for a while. But one day at work, he snapped. He'd gotten mad about some situation on the job and yelled at a customer or his boss. After that, he was terminated. He had trouble finding another job and ended up homeless.

The most disturbing thing about the story was that this man had the personal cell phone numbers for so many people at Children's Home and Youth Farm—including my own. He never called any of us because he was ashamed. I wasn't upset at him. If anything, I was upset at myself.

But I was grateful for the second opportunity to help.

After getting him dressed and cleaned up, I reached out to a friend and found him a place to stay with one of his distant relatives out of state. I got in touch with my team and the local Sheriff's Department and we bought him a one-way-ticket to get to his relative along with a little spending money. I walked him to the bus when it was time to leave and asked him not to get off until it had reached its destination.

As it drove off, I thought it might be the last time I ever saw or heard from him. But I was wrong.

Now every year on Father's Day, I get a call from him. He hasn't been back in trouble in a decade and he's started his own family. He's doing well for himself. He has a job and friends. He's made his own life. He's fulfilled the dream that Children's Home has for all our kids, that they might overcome whatever they've been through to become tax-paying citizens and members of society in good standing.

It's the dream that they can be in a position to realize their own dreams.

Looking at that story, I truly think I was meant to be there that day. I never go to lunch at that restaurant, and the timing couldn't have been more perfect. It was meant to be, for both of us. But above all, it was meant to be for him, because I truly believe that our encounter that day saved his life.

I tell potential employees and new donors all the time that we save lives and change lives, but it's different to hear a story like this and to see it happen in front of you. But I have 1,000 stories like that.

When I meet new employees, I tell them all kinds of stories. Like I said, of the 1,000 I have in my head, 500 are good and 500 are bad. From that bank of experience, I say that if someone tells you this business is 100 percent great, they're lying to you. But even if there are hard times and sad stories, you can still wake up every day willing to run through a wall to help other people—and I do.

That's the attitude I want people to have. I want them to do a lot of good for a lot people. If you have that attitude and will, you'll go far in our business. I want everyone to see on orientation day that I'm one of the speakers. I want them to see that I don't care about titles when it comes to taking care of people.

It's about your heart. That's how I sell what we do. The hard part is taking all of that complexity and channeling it all by picking the right story. Because once you do that, you can start encouraging other people to tell their own stories as well.

Not everyone is a great storyteller, but that doesn't matter. It's about showing people what's in your heart and understanding the exponential impact that has on other people. There are a lot of tough stories in this business, and most people come in not knowing what they don't know, essentially. It's rough when they get smacked in the face with reality, and suddenly they *do* know what's going on around them.

How they react to that and how they process that dictates how they will be as employees. The same is true for potential donors as well. While you can't completely remake a person's worldview, there are always people who want to help and to understand.

And the key to accessing that part of people is picking the right stories.

Chapter 9:
Mergers and Collaboration

Being "The Merger Guy"

Without a doubt, there are plenty of places where the nonprofit sector is just as cutthroat and competitive as any for-profit industry. We face all kinds of unique difficulties and the space is changing all the time. Still, the spirit of social service and nonprofit work is not to look sideways at other people like you who are just trying to help.

As a social service nonprofit, anybody in your community that's offering help to those in need, and has been for a long time, is a potential ally. It's easy to get trapped in a hyper-competitive mindset when the resources seem scarce, but I suggest another approach.

In a lot of situations, the most radical thing to do is to be "the merger guy." At least, that's what I've been a number of times throughout my career.

To really paint the picture, I have to go way back to when I was a young adult and had just broken away from working with my cousin to go out on my own in the nonprofit sector. A few years after leaving the Jeff George Foundation, I started my next big job as President and CEO of Youth Farm.

As I mentioned, Youth Farm is a residential program for kids. It was a relatively small program, but it was a great asset to the community. Still, because Youth Farm had a pretty small capacity, we were in a precarious position when it came to funding and competition with other nonprofits.

We had a good program, but there were other programs that were bigger. What we were offering was great, but it was niche and not particularly scalable. I was about 35 when I was running the program and was aware of all the risks we were facing. Meanwhile, not far from us was Children's Home, a much larger organization. From an outside perspective, they were a healthier, larger agency with more diverse programs.

In the process of working at Youth Farm for a few years, I started realizing that we were at risk in a few key ways. And I also realized that it was in Youth Farm's best interest to look for a partner. Shortly after that realization, I decided to go directly to Children's Home to start the conversation about joining forces.

This was a full-blown merger, and there were plenty of people around me that thought it was a crazy idea. From an ego-based perspective, merging with Children's Home was a tough personal decision. We were conceding to them on some level—but that's not how I saw it. I discussed the idea with my board members at Youth Farm and everyone gradually agreed that it was the right decision. Children's Home was six to seven times bigger than we were. They weren't going anywhere. Budget-wise, it seemed like it would be best for the kids and for the legacy and brand of Youth Farm to merge and call it a day.

What made the whole thing a little more unorthodox, though, was that I was walking directly towards my own termination as President and CEO of Youth Farm.

After approaching Children's Home, it was clear there would be organizational shake-ups from joining forces. The clinical staff would stay in place but some of the executive team would be absorbed and some people would become redundant. I just happened to be one of those people. That was one of the cost savings of the merger.

It was obviously not the easiest decision to make.

On the one hand, it would mean I would be unemployed as the President and CEO of an agency. On the other, it would mean that Youth Farm would have many more resources at its disposal. It could reach so many more kids who needed the help and the support.

It was clearly the right thing to do, no matter how much of a blow to my ego it would be. After some deliberation, the merger proceeded, and Youth Farm merged into Children's Home as a program rather than a separate entity. After that, I stepped away—there was another CEO already in place and she was doing a great job.

The result was a lot of kids were helped and I was out of a job—but I learned so many huge lessons from that decision. Before long, I had donors and politicians from all over the state calling me and congratulating me on making the decision that was ethically right for the community.

"What you did was the true definition of selflessness and it will come back tenfold for you," a state senator said when he called to applaud my decision. "And it'll come back a hundredfold for your community."

I missed Youth Farm, but I left a better person and a better man. I knew it was right for the kids and for the community. I had to look for an opportunity, but I didn't realize I was becoming the merger guy.

After Youth Farm merged with Children's Home and I stepped down, I started looking in the community for another position. Because Peoria is a relatively small town, most of the bigger fish in the area already had their executive teams in place. Instead, I had to look at some smaller agencies and programs to see where there might be a place for me. Before long, I found a position as the Executive Director of the Cancer Center for Healthy Living in Peoria.

The Cancer Center had been around a while and had offered services to people battling that dreaded disease in and around Peoria. The focus areas were mental health and healthy living. I came onboard in 2008 and brought my knowledge from Youth Farm. Right away I saw that though the people at Cancer Center for Healthy Living were doing great work, we could do more.

Our offices were in the same building as the Hult Health Education Center, though it was run separately. Both the Cancer Center and the Hult Center were small agencies, but they both offered great services to the community. I saw right away that there was a chance to join forces yet again, to restructure multiple organizations and negotiate some mergers to save money and get stronger—but I was a little bit worried about it.

I was thinking: "Here I go again, the merger guy coming in to shake up these companies." Nobody wants to change the way they're doing things—they think things are fine. Still, I'm a big believer in constantly improving, in collaborating and in doing the right thing above all. I saw right away that the right thing for the community would be to join these agencies together under one name.

We did it, and the fact was there were so many more efficiencies that formed by joining the agencies. In every merger I've been associated with, there have been both back office efficiencies and front-facing efficiencies. When you merge agencies together, you only have one director in charge of all of them—that's one salary instead of two. And all that additional money can get kicked back into the programs!

After we combined, I became the CEO of the Hult Center for Healthy Living.

I can truly say that I've lived the collaborative lifestyle, because I'm the only one in Peoria's social service sector who has orchestrated multiple mergers. I'm also the only one who actually stepped down as president for the good of the community. The beauty of it all was that it came full circle. After working at Hult Center for a few years, the CEO job at Children's Home became available again.

I applied, moved into the role and am still there today.

Creative Problem-Solving

The point of all of this is not to brag. It's to highlight the benefits and strengths of creative problem solving.

When it comes to being creative with very few dollars, nonprofits get some credit and they definitely deserve it. But to be a little controversial, what I'm saying is that a lot of the time, what nonprofits are doing isn't truly creative—they're just stretching their employees or their programs to the breaking point!

That's not creative thinking, that's subpar leadership.

True creative problem-solving means combining heads and forces. It means looking at the big picture with another organization and saying, "If you're helping 100 people and I'm helping 100 people, how can we combine to help 250?" It's all about finding an economy of scale, and a lot of times, people don't want to explore that. In those situations, executives can make decisions from a fear-based perspective. They're worried about what the board thinks or they're afraid of losing their jobs. Ultimately, they're worried about all the wrong things.

That's what I mean about true collaboration. Even though nonprofits are in competition with all kinds of agencies, it doesn't mean they can't collaborate. If local nonprofits aren't working with the school districts and other social service agencies, sometimes it can feel like they're just doing things to do things.

Organizations end up expending a lot of effort and a lot of resources to get outcomes that aren't as good as they could be. Different groups of people in your community will have different needs, and sometimes there's a need for multiple organizations. Still, more often than not, it's just egos protecting one sandbox, or getting in the way of providing better outcomes for everyone involved.

When it comes right down to it, there are some hard questions to face that don't have great answers. Are we ever going to completely get rid of poverty just through collaboration? Probably not. But are there ways to help people by working together? Definitely.

142 · MATT GEORGE

That's what I mean by getting on the same page within a community.

Obviously, every community faces its own unique issues. If you're reading about social issues in California, a lot of it has to do with the homelessness crisis in LA and San Francisco. For our part, homelessness isn't taking over in Peoria, Illinois. But we have other problems.

What's happening in Central Illinois has to do with community and education. There's sometimes a truancy problem. We have to work together to get kids out of the system, get them in school and to get them educated. But we have kids who aren't getting breakfast in the morning, or don't have access to uniforms, clean clothes or clean water. Education becomes priority 15 on the list when a child wakes up in the morning hungry or cold.

It all goes back to the main social issue of taking care of other people. It's about the coordination of care, which is so often the elephant in the room in all kinds of institutions—healthcare, nonprofits, you name it. It's hard to get a large organization of people on the same page and to get them all coordinated enough to produce great outcomes.

But it's also why a systemic approach and a collaborative culture are so important.

A big problem is that a lot of groups say they "collaborate" in the community, but don't. In the worst cases, they become a stagnant presence in the community—and maybe it's not an agency, maybe it's just a program. When a group of people have done something the same way for 15 years, they don't see any reason to change. But that's not the path to excellence.

If you look at a Fortune 500 company like McDonald's, you're going to find very few products that they haven't changed or tweaked over the years. At the very least, they've tweaked the systems behind them to make the production process more efficient.

Nonprofit organizations shouldn't be any different.

The world around us is always changing, and we have to change with the times. In the case of the social service sector, true collaboration is one of the answers to that problem.

Optimize the Community's Resources

There are different leadership styles at every organization, and some people are more open to collaboration than others. That's natural and understandable, but the stakes are a little different in the nonprofit sector. For us, collaboration is a strategy to optimize the community's resources. And the cost for not doing it can be great.

When nonprofits are only competing with one another for the same resources and not open to collaboration, it means that some of them will die out and close. When programs or agencies close, it puts more stress on the remaining agencies. If another children's agency has 200 kids a year flowing through their doors and it closes, they're not going to simply shut all those kids out in the cold.

Instead, they're going to reroute those kids to other agencies before they close up shop. The problem is those other agencies might not have the capacity or the personnel to deal with those kids. Though the other agencies might be able to grow and find a way to fund more programs, that process takes time—and the entire problem can be avoided with careful collaboration.

Right now, one of the biggest issues in the non-profit space is the duplication of services. There are plenty of places where there are 10 after school programs at 10 different agencies across town, all for the same population. Maybe each one of those has a good mission—they essentially all have the same mission—but now you have 10 stagnating programs instead of one thriving one.

With that being said, there are plenty of situations where multiple programs for the same thing are necessary. In terms of foster care, for example, sometimes the need for services is so high that it pays to have multiple agencies doing it. Still, there are plenty of areas where there's an excess of programs and a waste of resources—and that's when things get "competitive."

The programs that exist in those spaces start taking a compartmentalized approach to problem solving.

They become nepotistic, relationship-based or ego-driven. They argue amongst themselves: "You shouldn't be doing that; you're playing in my sandbox!" Of course, every agency is probably guilty of doing this a little bit from time to time.

But it pays to take a breath and examine why this is happening and how to change it.

Much like the situation with Youth Farm, sometimes a policy of non-competition and willful removal from the situation can work best for the community. Apart from the goals of one individual nonprofit, community improvement is always the ultimate goal.

A situation like that happened to Children's Home once when we applied for a $60,000 grant. I knew it was a lot of money and it could help us out, but I didn't know what other organizations were in the running. I went in to make a pitch, but never made it past the lobby. I saw that a bunch of representatives from smaller agencies that were also doing good work were competing for the same money.

Relatively speaking, we were the biggest fish in that room.

As soon as I saw that, I willingly withdrew Children's Home from the running. Trying to win that grant would've come off as pure greed. The other agencies were offering services we didn't, and we had a bigger operating budget already. We could've used the money, sure, but the other agencies needed it more.

I would've second-guessed myself if we'd actually gotten the grant.

Another suggestion for radical cooperation is to help other nonprofits in the community make money if possible. My relationship with my board is so strong that I'll sometimes even volunteer my time to fund-raise for other nonprofits or causes they value. Though these organizations aren't strictly our competition, there's an argument to be made for how they could be.

This may seem like a strange thing to suggest, but it's part of what makes nonprofit leadership different than for-profit leadership. It's not about you the individual or about the individual nonprofits. It's about the community.

Look at it this way: If you're a CEO running a program at a C- level, as a leader, do you really want to be in that position? Maybe it's not your fault that it's a sub-optimal program, but it is your responsibility to fix it. Maybe there's a chance to look across town to another program that's running at an A+ level to see if there's a chance to combine forces. Maybe both of you could run at a B+ in the short term before making it back up to an A.

But maybe it means giving up a little of your own power and giving up a little of your own security. That's where you start losing people.

My question to other CEOs and executives is: In a sector that is already stretched thin and dealing with limited resources, what do you want to be known for? If you could keep your job for five years by taking the community's resources and using them inefficiently, is that what you would really want to do?

The answer for me is no.

You have to evolve on a weekly basis in this business. You have to be open to new ideas and open to working with people. Otherwise, you become a stagnant mission or a dead program.

And that's where we're not like other businesses.

You can't tell a kid who needs help "no." You can tell a customer that your product is out of stock or it's on backorder, but you can't tell that to a homeless kid. Whether we're talking about truancy, homelessness, justice system reform or whatever else, there's a limited amount of resources to go into fixing these huge issues. And we need to maximize the community's resources to do so.

It's a vicious cycle, and that's definitely part of the problem. But another part of it is that nonprofits must do a better job at collaborating.

Chapter 10:
Building Legacy

Nonprofits Work in Generational Impact

Generally speaking, I have a handful of key ideas about nonprofits that I speak on all the time. The major one is that nonprofits are real businesses and not just programs. Another is that the best organizations are mission-based in a very tangible way, not an abstract way. Following from that, you need to keep your ego to a minimum and treat everyone equally within your organization to be successful.

Finally, you need to foster a culture of collaboration with other nonprofits rather than just competing all the time and wasting resources.

Still, all of these interlocking pieces lead to a powerful underlying message about the vision of nonprofits. And that's the simple fact that nonprofits don't work in quarterly profits. They work in generational impact.

No matter what position a person may hold at a nonprofit, it's important that they keep the idea of their agency's legacy in mind in everything they do. That person should feel honored and blessed to be a part of the living history of the organization. On the one hand, the organization at large has an obligation to uphold their brand and their reputation in the community, and to keep that honorable. But on the micro-level, each individual should do their best to represent that brand as well.

When I look at Children's Home, I'm not just thinking about my tenure and my ideas for making things better. I'm not even thinking just about my team, either. I'm thinking about the organization's 153-year history, of all the employees who have passed through its doors over the years. I'm thinking about all of the kids and families that our employees have helped, how many of those kids still live in the community and how many of them have families that are giving back in their own ways to this day.

Although it's easy to forget our history, if you go all the way back to 1866, a bunch of decisions that those women made to help the needy still inform so much of what we do today. What they did back then has shaped our community in a positive way.

It all mattered, even if they couldn't be here to see the final outcomes of their actions.

In the same way, I want to encourage everyone else to think about how what they're doing in the present matters as well. It matters now and it matters for the future.

In the case of our organization, being humble and understanding that we're there for the kids is the overall goal. Obviously, I understand that everyone wants to build a personal legacy, no matter what their position. If you're going to dedicate your life to a career or a calling, you want to feel like you've left your stamp on the world and that you've made a mark somehow. In a lot of cases, that's why people get into this business in the first place.

Regardless, the overall focus should be on the long-term—not the short-term. To make that even clearer, sometimes that means taking a business loss from a quarterly standpoint on certain programs if it's for the good of the community and the organization at large.

If you're in a for-profit business, there are plenty of things you wouldn't do that nonprofits do all the time. For example, if you found out that you had a program that was bleeding money, the obvious decision would be to slash the program.

Still, that logic doesn't extend to the service sector—with some caveats.

In some cases, we'll take a financial loss on a specific program for a lot of reasons. Maybe we're not sure how to optimize it yet, but in the short-term it's helping a lot of people. In other situations, sometimes it's worth continuing because even if we're losing in one area, the positive results from that program end up becoming an investment in another program.

The key to understanding that shift is in realizing that everything is connected at nonprofit agencies. Children come in with issues that extend to all different programs and cutting one will necessarily affect all the others negatively as well.

You can't do anything in isolation. It's all part of a larger system.

In fact, the reason I stress collaboration so much is that it's a good safeguard against cutting a program and essentially taking a step backwards from a community standpoint. There are plenty of times when an agency may bite off more than it can chew, and it's running a program that is losing money or isn't working in the long-term.

Rather than throwing your hands in the air, I would suggest that's a perfect opportunity for open communication and collaboration with other agencies. On the other hand, when collaboration isn't possible, that's also why I stress the importance of having at least some cash on hand (or your "rainy day fund," if possible) at all times that isn't tied up in various expenses.

All of these decisions about whether to do something with a short-term or a long-term goal are made quarterly and yearly. Frankly, they're made all the time. But one of the biggest questions becomes: Does our agency have the *capacity* to make those decisions? If you're not well organized and you're not managing your finances properly, facing shortages or scarcity will just mean that you're able to help fewer people.

And that's a situation you should avoid at all costs. If you're really mission-based, you're also focused on generational impact. The two things go hand in hand.

Legacy in Our Communities

While it's important for the executive team and the staff to understand the mission and the generational approach, it's equally important for your community to understand it. The fact of the matter is your organization's brand or personal legacy doesn't exist in isolation from the community. The community is an intrinsic part of it all.

It's for those reasons that I stress the importance of an active CEO and an open-door CEO. You want someone who is welcoming, inviting and curious. Someone who is compassionate about the lives of the people around them, who's out there shaking hands and meeting people and looking to bring the next new donors into the fold.

You want to impart the message that you're all in it together, and it's a message that goes beyond money. If you're at a fundraiser or a promotional event and you don't get quite as much money as you'd hoped for, that's one thing. But if you leave the room without having spread your mission and your message to everyone, that's a serious problem.

To that point, spreading legacy in the community isn't something that you can tackle all at once. As it turns out, it's often better accomplished through a lot of little gestures done over time.

For my part, I write more personal notes and thank you letters than anybody I know. I spend a lot of time talking to board members and to donors, thanking them for their wisdom, guidance and generosity. When it comes to my team, I want everyone to be better and I want them all to learn as much as they can about our industry.

To that end, I buy somewhere in the neighborhood of 100 to 125 books a year to give out as gifts to my team. In each one, I'll write a personal note, maybe highlight some sections and get them in the hands of the people who can use their wisdom.

Just like not always focusing on your balance sheet shows that you have big picture thinking, these kinds of thoughtful gestures show goodwill. They show that you have integrity and that you care about the people around you. Even if buying all those books to give out or writing all those letters seems frivolous or excessive, it really is an investment in the goodwill of the community and of your team.

In its own way, making time for small acts of kindness is an investment in your brand. And those kinds of behaviors are impressive to donors.

Keeping your eyes on the big picture and not getting unnecessarily bogged down in details are ultimately good for your business anyway. After all, building generational impact begins and ends with community.

So, it's your duty to give as much back to the community as you possibly can.

Legacy in Our Families

Though I talk a lot about legacy on the broader scale, the truth is there's a very personal part of what legacy means to me as well. And it has to do with my family.

I have five kids, four daughters and one son. My three daughters Carly, Allie and Lauren are older—they're 25, 23 and 20 years old. The younger two are Izzie and Matthew, and they're nine and eight. When I was younger and I was first getting into this business, I made sure to get my kids involved. I wanted them to understand what I was doing and why (within reason). I would go to the office on the weekends and take them with me. Other times, I'd take them on-site to the facilities to meet the kids and to see what was going on.

Although I didn't want to tell my family too many of the gritty details about the work we were doing, I did want them to have a sense of perspective about their own lives. I wanted them to learn to be sensitive to the world around them and not to shut their eyes to it. When they came home to our house, I wanted them to think, "Man, I'm lucky."

My kids work at any fundraising event I do. I require it.

But as a young dad, I was naïve. I was doing social service work, but in the back of my head, I was thinking I wanted my kids to grow up to be doctors and lawyers and so on—any professional career that fit into the stereotype of success. Like any dad, I wanted to spare them from pain, and I wanted them to have an easier life than I had, whatever that meant.

But my plans for my oldest kids never came to fruition.

Instead, my oldest daughter Carly called me one day and said, "Dad, I took an internship at a residential treatment center in Chicago." I was shocked. Even though I'd been laying the groundwork for an interest in social service my whole life, I guess on some level I didn't think it would take—or at least, I didn't want to force anyone into it.

I had mixed feelings about it. On the one hand, I was so proud of Carly for her decision. On the other, I knew how hard the road ahead would be.

Sure enough, she called me crying a few days later after working in the trenches at her new job. Seeing what the people there were going through had put our life and my career, the details of which I'd kept hidden from my family, into plain view.

"I didn't know," she said to me on the phone between tears. "Why didn't you tell me? Why didn't you tell me this is what you do? I just didn't realize the emotion and empathy that this job would bring out."

I explained to her that when she was a little girl, I could never tell her the exact specifics of what I did. I never thought she'd get into the same business, and I'd wanted to protect her. Still, those early lessons in compassion and perspective had paid off—here she was as an adult walking the same path.

I should've had more faith in my daughter in the first place, because all her new experiences only made her tougher. After working that job for some time, she got a letter from a little boy that basically said that she'd saved his life. That letter changed my daughter.

For lack of a better way to put it, it made her realize the power of just being a human being.

After that internship, she graduated from college, decided to get her master's and told me she was going to be a school-based therapist. She just graduated with her master's recently and got started in the behavioral health world. On one level, I never pictured her doing this work—but I couldn't be prouder of her.

And the pattern didn't stop there.

My second oldest, Allie, is a super outgoing girl and a complete joy to be around. Sure enough, she also got an internship in behavioral health and social services, this time at a place that helped adults with disabilities. That was two summers ago, and that experience changed her life as well. She later went to the University of Iowa and got her degree in therapeutic recreation. The main question she's always asking as an adult is: "What can I do to help others?"

Out of all of that experience, she's been helping senior citizens with the dream of one day working for the Special Olympics.

My third oldest daughter Lauren is still in school, but she wants to work with and take care of children. There is no doubt Lauren is following in the same footsteps and will one day make a big impact. My two youngest aren't quite at that stage in life yet, but whatever they do, the chances seem pretty good that they'll be interested in giving back to others.

If I went a decade back in time, I never would've thought that this is the path my daughters would've chosen for themselves. But after mulling it over a bit more, now I'm thinking: Why *wouldn't* they choose that path?

For starters, they all have big hearts on their own. But secondly, they all got to see from a very young age what it feels like to help others and to change people's lives—and the key word there is *feel*.

For me personally, I live everything I preach because the legacy of Children's Home and—more broadly—of service, lives on through my family. My kids got to know what it feels like to make a difference in people's lives when they were very little. Most people don't get to feel that fully until they're well into their careers—and some people don't ever get to feel it at all.

I may have once thought I wanted my kids to be lawyers or something else, but that's not what we do. The George family legacy is that we help people.

We change lives and save lives

Chapter 11:
Conclusion

Every Child Is Their Own Case Study

Whenever I talk about nonprofits and working in service, I get fired up. Though a lot of the work I do is focused on the fine details, a major part of my job is focusing on the big picture and helping other people stay focused on it as well. But the last thing there is to talk about is how you connect the big picture to the granular one.

And I'll start by putting it simply: every child is his or her own case study.

When you work in social services, you butt up against a lot of big philosophical questions. One big question is about causality, and it's one that people tend to get hung up on. There's a line of thinking that says if people are down and out or need help, they earned what they're getting. It's along the same lines of thinking as the belief that those who are poor chose to be poor, or bad things happen to people because they deserve them.

I reject that outright. But what I will say is that the world is changing very fast, and with those shifts, a lot of old bonds of community are getting weaker. You can point at culture, technology, bad food, a broken justice system or whatever you want. But the bigger point is that it's being driven by a lot of factors that are huge and beyond any one person's scope.

Still, it's a massive problem that can be answered directly through service.

The work we do at Children's Home gets done at a very intimate level. It's a one-to-one process, and it has a lot to do with rebuilding the bonds of community and family at a very local scale. And from a chain of those little efforts and little repairs, what starts to emerge is an interconnected network of good outcomes—that's a community. But to build that bigger chain of community, you have to look at each link individually.

In this case, the links in the chain are the kids and the families we serve. And no two of them are exactly alike.

As recently as 10 years ago, if you had a focus area or a set program with 50 kids in the program, the philosophy could be to label all those kids as one thing. They would have a certain common diagnosis and be pigeonholed into some treatment area.

Fortunately, that seems to be changing.

Over time, behavioral health has expanded and become more nuanced. The categories and labels that we put on people are getting more specific and less rigid. In some senses, the labels have disappeared—and that's definitely a good thing.

Everything is becoming more individual, and nonprofits are gradually realizing that. If you're running an autism program, for example, you can't look at those 50 kids and say they're all autistic and leave it at that. You can't treat those 50 kids the same way, even if they all fit a certain definition—even if it's the same diagnosis. Each of those cases has its own tendencies and its own needs.

To put it more bluntly, none of those cases is a figure on a spreadsheet. Each one is a person and an individual.

At Children's Home, we have 1,700 kids and family members per month that go through our agency. Within that picture are 1,700 different personalities, 1,700 different names and 1,700 different identities. You just can't lump people together like that. The best stories to me are the ones where a family comes to us for help and they have 50 different complex issues to deal with, but we find a way to meet their needs—through sophisticated and coordinated care.

Out of a good treatment plan like that, the outcome can be a productive tax-paying citizen who is integrated into society again. That sounds like it's putting a monetary value on what we do, but it's not about that.

The point is that it builds community. For a lot of people, the best medicine for depression or anxiety is to be able to go out and work. The difference is sometimes the people we help truly can't go get work for whatever reason. Bridging that gap makes a huge difference.

When they walk out our doors, a lot of these kids become adults, get out of the system and set off to start their own families. Maybe they even open businesses and give back to the community in some way. Some of them might even come volunteer at Children's Home or give back into the community in some other way.

On another level, there's never one single person who changes a kid's life. It's the work of a coordinated team, of a bunch of people working together. When the kids come in through our doors, plenty of them don't trust people.

They don't trust the system, because it has already failed them somewhere along the way.

From that perspective, we need to think about what we can do rebuild that trust. We need to think about finding the missing pieces of the puzzle. And there's no telling what the outcome of each case will be.

As I said, it makes every child his or her own case study.

We once had a young boy who was nonverbal. Over a two to three-year period of working with our team, he learned to communicate in ways he never had before. Although that was huge for the child, the bigger picture is how huge it was for his family. Because of our team's efforts, this boy and his mother were able to communicate with each other in ways they never had before.

It's hard to understand how important that is. It's a life-changing thing.

In the case of autism or developmental disabilities, each of the kids we help is on a completely different wavelength from one another, let alone the rest of us. Sometimes you'll see someone who makes slow, incremental progress over the course of years. Other times, you'll see kids who are in physically abusive situations and once they're removed from it, they blossom overnight. They become entirely new people.

Once kids finish our programs, it's hard to track them as adults. Sometimes they stay around the community and remain in touch with our staff, and sometimes they want to shake off the label of who they were.

Still, whenever we see these kids around town, we give them a kind look that says, "We've got you."

As I said before, the nonprofit world is full of a bunch of stories that end well and some that end badly. But getting mired down in arguments about how things got the way they are or who deserves to be helped will only distract you and slow you down.

The job is to help people to the best of your ability and to build community, no matter what. From that point of view, every child becomes his or her own case study, and you stay infinitely curious.

It's definitely hard work, and it's not for everybody. But it's some of the most satisfying work there is.

Compassion Can Be Taught

As I mentioned before, it takes a certain kind of person to get involved in nonprofit work in the first place. There are plenty of people who want to help the world out in some way, but the special combination of empathy and grit that it takes as an adult to do this work is relatively unique.

That makes it tempting to take an essentialist view of the work—to believe that some people are meant for service and some aren't.

I would push back against that a little bit. Even if there's an opinion out there that personalities are fixed and people can't change, I've found that compassion can definitely be taught.

In the case of my own children, they all had big hearts and grit to begin with, but they also had a special set of circumstances that led them to do what they do. They had me as their dad, and they had repeated exposure as children to the reality of what was going on around them.

Although I did my best to shield them from some of the things I thought they weren't ready for, they definitely got a taste of just how harsh the world can be. Just like any other complex issue like addiction or developmental disability, it's not just one thing or the other. It's a whole number of things.

Some people may be wired a little more towards drinking, but the environment they're in makes all the difference. Their habits become the result of something innate *and* their environment.

It's so tempting to think it's all innate, because it gives us license to give up on people. But that's just unrealistic and cruel thinking.

The fact of the matter is that gradual exposure to harshness over time can actually teach empathy, and it can help build a sense of legacy in family and community at the same time. In the same sense, gradual exposure over time to cruelty, neglect and so on will produce the opposite outcomes.

In both cases, you're working on a gradual sliding scale over a long period of time. And what you choose to do on that time scale to move the needle matters enormously.

In my head, I have a bunch of kids' faces that came to Children's Home distrusting us, suspicious of the system, from broken situations that would horrify and break potentially anybody. But I also know that through our team's efforts and through the kids' own grit, a lot of them turned those situations around dramatically.

When you're willing to help, there's no limit to what can be accomplished.

And to come full circle, my hope is that the compassion I helped to instill in my own children is the same sense of compassion I can instill in the kids who come through Children's Home. That's the real definition of community.

When you have a group of people who were left behind by a broken system, you pick them up and care for them. You give them what they need, and you teach them that the bad things don't define their life. There are also good people and good opportunities in the future—and it's a future that they have a hand in creating.

If you can keep that attitude in everything you do, there's no telling how far you can take it.

Where Do We Go from Here?

The bottom line is that nonprofits are here to stay and social service works—but there are still changes to be made and work to be done. The question I would pose to every person who wants to get into social service and to every nonprofit executive reading this book is: Where do we go from here?

Anyone who has actually worked helping others knows that this attitude and this kind of giving can change and save lives. We know it works because we've seen the results of our efforts firsthand. But how do we paint the picture? How do we move from the extremely specific cases to the huge, world-changing vision that is also hugely attainable?

For the people who have been there, I think the answer lies in telling stories and spreading your experiences far and wide. You already see that what you're doing works; now all you need to do is communicate it to other people.

For anybody who isn't sure how all this giving back is going to work or if it is going to work at all, I would recommend starting. Start right now.

It doesn't have to be anything huge, and it can be something that you do right in your backyard. Go down to your local church and help with a food drive. Start talking to the people in your community and get some information about what programs are already in place to help. Start thinking about your own skills and your own talents and think about how you might use them to make the world a better place.

One thing I would also add is that we should think of giving and service as a lifelong mission. When it comes to taking on the big problems of mental illness and poverty, nothing ever really ends. In a sense, you're always starting now. You're always starting at the very beginning.

Even after we've helped kids through all our programs and sent them out into the world as adults, the buck still never stops. If we see those kids in the community struggling with anything, they still have all our contact information and people just a phone call away. It's a long haul and it's hard work, but it always keeps things interesting.

Just as nonprofits work for positive generational impacts, all the social ills work for negative generational impacts. Both of those effects echo through the decades. In many cases, those echoes are running through all the institutions and communities all around us, and we don't always see exactly how they work.

Sometimes, they're affecting our families and friends negatively and we're very aware of their sting. But other times, we're on the positive side of the equation.

We're benefitting from having a good family around us, of having friends, of having a place to live. We take it for granted that the good effects we're experiencing are just what reality is, that everybody must be living this way. And anybody who doesn't fit that mental image we've created essentially becomes invisible to us.

That's exactly the thinking we have to rail against.

It's a raising of awareness. There are good and bad cycles in life, and everyone around us is going through them all the time. The world is not a perfect place, and it's made up of a lot of systems that produce a lot of pain for a lot of people. But we don't need to swallow the world whole.

We just need to focus on the systems and cycles that are right in front of us, the ones we know we can improve, and plant ourselves right in the middle of them.

Poverty, crime, mental illness and dissolving communal bonds are all hard problems to solve—and they're all vicious cycles. They all feed off of one another and they only get stronger by being ignored or denied. If we do nothing, they'll keep growing and they'll keep getting stronger. But those cycles can be interrupted and sometimes even broken, and anyone who works in the social service sector can assure you of that.

It's our duty to open our hearts and to stand in the middle of that cycle. No matter who you are or what you do, the mission of changing lives and saving lives is a universal one.

And the best part is everybody's welcome to join.

Acknowledgements

To my Dad—the idea of this book came to me because of what you taught me. I learned to be a CEO because of you. To my Mom—you are the strongest woman I have ever known. I got my toughness from you. I love you both so much.

To Mike—It has been 38 years since you have come into all of our lives. We all appreciate and love you so much.

To Lisa—you're such a smart businesswoman. Thank you for all that you do.

To Kevin Harrington—My mentor, my friend. I really can't thank you enough.

To Laura—You are the best. We lead a very busy and hectic life, but you're always there for us. I could not do anything without you. Love you.

To Carly, Allie, Lauren, Izabelle, and Matthew — Nothing in life makes me prouder than to be your Dad. You are all so special. I love you more than you will ever know.

To Andy, Kathy, and Becky — We have the strongest bond and you three will be and are my best friends, brothers and sisters. Love you all.

To my cousin Jeff — "The Sheriff." You mean so much to me. We have done a lot and I know we still will do more. Love you Sheriff.

To Brent, Collin, and Justin — Very proud of you three. You all have artistic talent that is so impressive. You amaze me with it.

To Senator Chuck Weaver — Your mentorship for the past 20 years has made me a better businessman, person, and family man. Thank you so much.

To Chief Michael McCoy — I've learned a lot from you. As tough as you are, you are even more compassionate. That's a real talent.

To Patti Bash — My "Peoria Mom." Nobody has a heart like you. We all strive to be that person who is always giving, always smiling.

To Ken Snodgrass—One of the most dedicated people I know to a cause. You have given me thoughts and advice I will always cherish and appreciate. The past 18 years you have made me stronger and a better leader. Thank you.

To Ryan Aliapoulios—You are a great talent and I appreciate all of your help. I'm very impressed.

To Kristen McGuiness—How you got into my head and sorted things out so quickly I will never know. You have a special gift.

To Anna David—You are a Rock Star. I couldn't have done any of this without you giving me a chance.

To the Children's Home team—I have been so blessed to work with such great people. The hard work and dedication is unreal. We change lives and save lives.

To the Children's Home Board, members past and present—We have the best people any leader could ask for. I've learned more from all of you than from anything I've done in my life. You all give your time and talents to better the kids and families of our awesome community.

To the city of Danville, Illinois—I was lucky to grow up in Danville. It is a great place to live.

To the City of Peoria, Illinois—I could not be any prouder to be part of such a great community. Peoria is my *home*, and that will never change.

To contact Matt George directly concerning appearances, speaking engagements, or consulting/coaching, please contact him at matt@themattgeorge.com.

Contact or follow Matt George on:
Twitter: @themattgeorge
Facebook: @themattgeorge
Instagram: @therealmattgeorge
LinkedIn: the-matt-george

For more information or to make a donation to the Children's Home Association of Illinois, please visit *www.chail.org* or send to Children's Home Association of Illinois, 2130 N Knoxville Avenue, Peoria, Illinois 61603.